# WHEN SONGBIRDS
# RETURNED TO PARIS

## E.M. SLOAN

Paris 2002.
*Elizabeth Sloan*

FAWKES PRESS

Design by Michelle Fairbanks/Fresh Design
Edited by Pamela Yenser


PRINT ISBN 978-1-945419-04-1
EPUB ISBN 978-1-945419-05-8
Library of Congress Control Number: 2015920252

# TABLE OF CONTENTS

To my daughter, Margot, who has the
independent and intrepid Humble spirit
coursing through her bloodline.

And for Cecily: your presence was—
and is—an imperative to peace. *Merci.*

*Every soul is a melody*
*which needs renewing.*

—Stéphane Mallarmé

# PART ONE

# THE FRENCH DOSSIER

Author (right) and Cecily Spiers at Chateau de Vincennes,
Ministry of Defense, Paris, France.
*Margot Gildner*

An average person on an average day awakens sensibly. One tumbles out of bed easily, while another bolts to the cymbal of an alarm bell; one ascends to a calming melody, leaps toward a baby's plea, greets an unexpected phone call, or answers the urgent need to relieve oneself. Most—at four o'clock in the morning—simply give a squinted glance to the time, rotate to the other shoulder, listen for a moment to the surging aria of birdsong at this universal hour of their awakening, and nestle back into the covers of repose for as long as they can put off the inevitable beginning of another day. Not many give a fleeting thought to where birdsong no longer exists, to mornings of what, for some terrifying years, was a signature of the Holocaust: *l'appel*. Roll call.

# I. NOUS COMMENÇONS

Cecily Margot Gordon and Chow.
*Author's collection*

# WE BEGIN

Margaret Humble Close, mother of Cecily,
when she was presented to court.
*Author's collection*

**MY NAME IS CECILY MARGOT GORDON LEFORT.** That much is true. I have been dead now for almost seventy years, and it occurs to me that for this story to be told, I must first capture your attention.

It was a time of war. Staying alive within the confines of a German concentration camp was not simple. Or perhaps so simple, that but for one unfortunate final decision, I might have survived. If that were so, I would not be telling the story you are about to hear.

Toward the end of the war, many of us realized we would probably not live to tell our own stories. This possibility became one of our main concerns. Who would validate us? Who would live to hold our enemy accountable? We believed that each of our journeys was worth telling, a rationale attached to individual recognition, something the Nazis tried quite diligently to deny.

I felt alone at the time. I suppose it would be fair to say I felt abandoned, though with the distinction that this does not mean I felt sorry for myself. I realize now that my sense of isolation was caused not only by the separation from my husband, my friends, and my countries (yes, both England and France), but also by the loss of even my false, secret identity. I was cut off from any reality that I knew. Even the songbirds were drowned out by cries of human suffering.

You may rightly wonder how I have been able to return—from the dead as it were—and speak now of these events. I didn't attempt my search for many years after my death, when the songbirds had returned, but I was no longer alive to hear their music.

My desire to make a connection was not just about that time of war. It was about all that had been going on outside me during that real time; the details that affected my life but that were outside my realm of awareness.

And so I reached out, through dreams, to an intuitive woman in Iceland who had an interest in historical events. We went on for years. She was making connections for me in that time after the war, connections about my husband and how life did go on. It was comforting to realize that I had not been forgotten.

But still, that was a one-way channel. The ripples of information did not satisfy my hunger to go deeper. It was during this time that a window opened. I say that metaphorically, but I also realize that a space quite literally opened. For the first time since I was captured as a secret agent, I heard the hint of birdsong. Someone was breaking through. Someone with a passion equal to mine. Someone with the same bloodline.

Finally, I am ready to tell my story.

Imagine now an antique drop-leaf table placed behind a pastoral upholstered loveseat. On this table, among porcelain figurines and brass candleholders, is a photograph of me propped on a brass easel: I am the small girl sitting atop a furry black Chow. My right foot is turned slightly outward as if I have just lighted upon my favorite pet and been told to "hold still, darling" so my image can be taken. I sit very still as I've been told (but still ready to take off, should my Chow lose his patience) and stare into the camera lens. My image is captured and displayed as a child forever in a red tooled-leather picture frame, edged with detailed bars of gold borders.

And so I have been, up to this day, framed and displayed, packed and moved, held on to tightly during trials and tribulations, for all those years that followed the snap of the shutter. I can only hope that my captured stoic posture provided some measure of comfort to my mother as she rode out the storm that surrounded so much of our lives.

Somehow my small-framed image passed between family hands for the next few generations. The image has faded a bit. The frame is worn and frayed from handling, and the time is 95 years henceforth. The setting is the middle of North America and here now is another young woman with a child of her own, gazing at me through the thin layer of glass. This mother's name is Elizabeth. I shall call her Lizzie.

"Who is the child in this photograph?" Lizzie asks her own mother more than once.

"That is your grandmother's cousin, Cecily Close. She was a spy during WWI and helped British pilots escape from France. She was executed."

(Stay with me, now. These misleading "facts" will be addressed soon enough.)

Because Lizzie's child is the same age as I was in the photograph, this mother acquires an ardent interest in me: a pale child with a tangle of fine curly hair sitting atop the tangle of a black furred dog as large as the little girl. A spy? Executed? How can this be? Lizzie contemplates.

One can certainly imagine the ideas of subterfuge and compromise this image would summon.

The contemporary child's name is Margaret, the fourth Margaret in the family, my mother being the first, as far as this story is concerned. We all thread up from the energy of my mother, just the same. But more about family names is yet to be revealed.

As this dichotomy between child and "spy" takes root in Lizzie's mind, my life, in so many enlightening ways, is at last revived. The photo inset slips out of the leather frame, and had Lizzie looked more closely, she might have noticed the barely legible writing of Cecily Gordon, and the year 1901, penciled in beneath the Alfred Ellis & Walery Photographers address at 51 Baker Street in London. If she had, the journey she is about to embark on might have taken a more direct route. But as it is, with only those three sentences to identify me (bearing the wrong name, the wrong war, the wrong endeavor), an international journey of discovery is set in motion.

I have come to this moment to tell my story—I must trust, dear reader, your ability to suspend disbelief and persevere—along with so much that Lizzie's curiosity, yes even bordering on obsession, comes to reveal.

Only now am I able to fully comprehend the fact that I indeed do not even have a grave.

My death most likely occurred in early spring of the year 1945. You see, even I am not sure. Murder was not yet a label applied to these historic events. There is no exact record of my death, though much has been investigated as to the day, or even month, in the elusive records from the end of this war. It was in fact my second war; the first one, the one that history declared would be "the war to end all wars," did no such thing.

I suppose it was my experience in the First War that in many ways led to my experience, and my death, in the Second War. With the beauty of hindsight from my current bird's-eye view, it was events of my childhood that in so many other ways laid out the course of my life.

And what would my childhood, or my entire life journey for that matter, have been, were it not for the story of my mother, that first Margaret in this lineage, with all her elegance and drama, in the life she lived before all that was to become "me"?

There are many beginnings to any story, just as there are sometimes many endings. One ending is fact, and inescapable: I died (though for quite some time, even that was debated). Other endings embrace conjecture: the journey toward the end. So I shall meander somewhere in the center of Mother and me for a while, with another photographic scene from my childhood. The implications in this English garden setting will take us back, then, to another beginning.

My name is Cecily Margot Gordon. It is, again, 1901, and I am nestled on my mother's lap with our three Chows. We are on the family grounds in Bayswater, England.

The day of the informal sitting beneath the Chestnut trees, Mother wears a pastel dress cascading with summer lace. Her lavish hair is loosely bound beneath the festooned brim of a straw hat. Perhaps humidity that day causes my untamed curls to flutter in all directions. Our three Chows pant in the heat, wanting only to escape to the shade beneath a canopy of ferns. But one image is managed, with Mother's face turned down in a contemplative gaze. The three furry Chows—two cinnamon and one black—encircle the filigreed hem of Mother's gown and must have tickled my toes so that a giggle escapes and flutters above our pets' perked ears like so many lace-winged butterflies.

As fate would have it, this is to be one of the last days enjoyed in that lush botanical scene. Another chapter in my mother's passionate and heartbreaking life is relentlessly developing. I should speak of my mother's husbands, and then her lover, as one of these is my father.

Mother's first husband was Frederic Close. Frederic and his brothers, William and James, were to become known as English Gentlemen Farmers. They settled Le Mars, the first British colony in a territory named Iowa, in the middle of the land of America. What an adventure that chapter of Mother's life had been.

Imagine the year 1876. It was an occasion of expansion and opportunity on the unclaimed land of tall grass prairie, harsh but fertile. The time was ripe for crossing the Atlantic from England to North America, rattling across the new continent by rail, and advancing just past the bluffs of the Missouri River, on into Iowa. A progeny of Redcoats had arrived, not as soldiers but as farmers, to settle an English colony on prairie land, established by these Close brothers.

Satisfied that the ten-year grasshopper plague had ended— thank goodness this unpleasant episode was over—many wealthy Englishmen realized the opportunity of investment in such potentially rich farmland. They arrived with adventurous spirits and financial patronage. Completion of the Chicago and Northwestern Railroad reassured them of a promising future.

Into this scene hastened a venerable English coterie, led by the Close brothers, and reinforced by my mother's family line, the Humbles. They brought cricket bats, croquet mallets, hunting dogs, and a number of race ponies with such names as Petrarch, Lady Grace, Ned, and Kitchen Maid, along with trunk-loads of fine china and silver service sets.

Sandwiched between months of hard labor that cultivating the farmland involved, these refined English gentlemen managed to arrange an array of lavish celebrations. Events such as cricket matches, polo tournaments, and parties in honor of any number of marriages and other occasions drew in hundreds of revelers. One of these events was the elaborate marriage ceremony of Mother and Frederic Close. One can imagine how distasteful this flurry of horse-drawn carriages and horn-blowing dance soirées might have appeared to the local "real" farmers.

Mother's retelling of our family's passage abroad, once I was of an appropriate age to understand such commerce, consumed my thoughts and filled my head with fanciful daydreams of her daring adventures of discovery. (Enticing new sights, sounds, smells, romance!)

Of this I am not certain: the particulars of how the Close and Humble families were acquainted. Perhaps they frequented the same social circles in London to be sufficiently familiar, so that my widowed Grandmama—Harriet Proudfoot Humble—placed full faith in the Close brothers' ability to stand in as respectable male figures to Mother's brother, Edward.

Grandmama was an independent and shrewd woman, perhaps by necessity for endurance. Under William and Frederic Close's guidance and with their encouragement from afar, Grandmama invested in prairie acquisitions. Edward, familiar name Teddy, soon set sail from England to join the bustling development of rural America and oversee our Humble family's landholdings. I can't help but believe that Grandmama's fortitude was itself a large influence on my mother's own adventurous spirit, which in turn surely inspired my life philosophy, to embrace chance rather than remain stagnant.

Be that as it may, the dust had not yet settled from Teddy's arrival in the middle of America, when ambitious Grandmama set sail from England. Her daughters Susan, Anne, and Margaret (my mother yet to be) accompanied her. They arrived upon this Western scene in a swish of pantaloons that, as Mother humorously recalled, literally billowed with the dry dusty wind that vacuumed across the fields of prairie grass.

A reason, now, for such ancestral references: I feel that to know me, and to appreciate the directions my life traveled, one must understand my background, at least to a minimal extent. I don't intend to soften the final outcome, for it was dark indeed. In order to understand the dark, you must know some of the light that shone upon much of my early life.

It is not my life alone that ended in that final vale of darkness, but the full and adventurous lives of many of my eventual acquaintances and fellow passengers on this journey as well, when the world and the war diverted our paths in such unlikely and uncharacteristic manners.

With such a large story still at hand, it is time to consolidate these family musings, as if you and I were having a conversation over cocktails and you were to say, "So, tell me about your mother. How did she inspire you?"

I shall summarize that episode of Mother's life for you, and I promise this interlude to be brief (time being relative).

My English mother, Margaret Humble, married a British Gentleman farmer, Frederic Close, on the prairies of North America sometime around 1880. He was handsome and adventuresome. He was also a champion polo player, which indeed provided a rugged, romantic presence. Ten years later, however, this sport led to his demise. In June 1890, racing (fool-heartedly?) with his arm in a sling from a previous break, Frederic fell from his horse during a steeplechase competition. Perhaps he was riding his brother William's spirited Thoroughbred stallion, Elsham. Most unfortunately, in spite of intensive efforts, Frederic died from the injuries. My mother soon returned to England where she was introduced into British society as beautiful, wealthy, and widowed.

Eligible bachelors soon pursued Mother's company, and she was officially presented to the court of Queen Victoria. Among the group of interested suitors was Christian Frederic Gordon, an eligible Scotsman of the clan Gordon, and the grandson of the ninth Marquis of Huntly. Familiarly called Eric, he coincidently was a distant relative to Frederic, my mother's first husband. Mother eventually conceded to Eric's declarations of affection, and they soon married, but while life is rarely simple, Mother seemed to hold a full deck of complications.

These relationship details were not often alluded to between Mother and me, but some of the events and subsequent life-affecting turns my childhood path took as a result are recorded for posterity in *Lord Reading and His Cases,* in a chapter titled "The Gordon Custody Case." I was indeed the subject of that custody controversy.

(I realize that this story is much too involved to be told over a glass of Cointreau at a cocktail party, so we must move the scene to a dinner table, perhaps over roast rabbit followed by bread pudding and cognac. Please, settle back, and stay the course.)

Eric Gordon's older cousin, Lord Granville Gordon, had won Mother's heart more than a year before she married Eric. Unfortunately, Lord Granville already had a wife.

This wife, Lady Granville Gordon, was perhaps the reason for all the Chows in our home, as she owned the first Blue Chow in England. Lord and Lady Granville's daughter, Lady Faudel-Phillips—Evelyn to family—established the famous Amwell Chow Chow Kennels in England. Evelyn continued their prize Blue Blood's line for nearly 25 years, until her death in 1942.

(Yes, I was notified when Evelyn passed along; after all, we did share the same father, even if legal papers didn't reflect this fact. And I have always been grateful for my childhood companions, those fiercely loyal Chows. But perhaps I've gotten ahead of the story. Read on!)

Apparently, the closest Mother could come to being with Granville was to marry Eric. According to her later testimony—under oath—the romantic arrangement between Granville and herself bore Eric's understanding, if not his blessing. The situation between Mother, Eric, and Granville (as Mother preferred to name him, rather than the jaunty name of Ginger that his boar-hunting friends called him), persevered for the next five years.

And then I was born.

Now at last I return to this opening garden setting, with Mother seated amid flora and fauna, afloat in a cloud of lace from the top of her picture hat to the lawn below, holding me on her lap with my Chow-tickled toes. Though I am barely two years old, I do have some vague awareness of the garden that day. I smell the humid aroma of honeysuckle, feel the dew-damp grass on my bare feet, and sense a tension in the air that I am too young to interpret, but just old enough to intuit the strain. Perhaps it is the impending leave of my home, my pets, my world as I have known it, that infuses me with an indelible memory through all of my senses that I absorb from the garden this day.

The day begins with a journey in the carriage into London, with Mother, one Chow, and myself. Perhaps Granville assists; this I don't recall, but if not Granville, then who captures that image of Mother and me in the family garden later this same day? We make our way to the Alfred Ellis & Walery photography studio on Baker Street. (To be fair, some of these details I glean from my future perspective as a young woman, asking Mother so many questions she takes leave of her graciousness.) This Baker Street location eventually becomes significant in those months leading up to my secret agent training, a detail that overcomes me during that later time of war like a blast of nostalgia.

It is after this rigorous studio session on Baker Street that Mother and I return to the garden and are caught in the impromptu image:

me, eager to be back in the comfort of a familiar setting; Chow-Chow happy to return to her playmates and food dish; and Mother, oh, Mother must be in emotional turmoil. Surely she realizes that this will be our last portrait taken from our home in England, knowing full well the direction our lives are soon to take.

I see already how memory fails me. My exact departure from England was still two years off, but undoubtedly that day in the garden represented the end of something in my consciousness. I won't go so far as to say the end of childhood innocence, for I clung to that like a life vest. The energy in our home must have changed, or darkened in some permeable way and washed over our world. The garden was not tended to in the usual way those following years. Even our Chows seemed to grow weary and irritated. I only recall that Mother lost her radiance and seemed to be elusive to my longing for attention for some time to come. Looking back, of course, I conjecture that the custody trial endeavors must have interfered with our day-to-day rhythms. No doubt Eric and Granville were at odds, which could not help but upset Mother's days, and nights.

I was a precocious child, or perhaps the odd familial circumstances encouraged this attitude, for I did not call either Eric or Granville "Poppa." I called them Eric and Granny. Looking back, it seemed that, while Granny at first felt my pet name for him took a toll on his masculinity, he soon warmed to the affectionate calling. Meanwhile, Eric, the cuckold in this threesome, resented the ease with which I related to his cousin, the rival for his wife's, and his child's, affections.

Mother claims—and this is documented in Lord Reading's court case—that Granny is my father. "Just look at the child," she is recorded as saying on the witness stand. "Why, anyone can see that she is Granville's." In the legal courts of England, however, Eric is recorded to be my father.

I had in my possession for years the Hearst news article that covered the trial. The entire incident was abstract enough to me at the time that I escaped being traumatized, and later rather looked upon the affair with girlish intrigue. A particular scene from the news issued on February 23, 1903 (I still recall the date, as I reviewed the article so often), especially rooted in my imagination: "The courtroom was filled with a brilliant throng. At each new and startling revelation, the female spectators seemed to murmur approval...Their lovely picture hats quivered with emotion." When I was finally mature enough to interpret this incident, I dearly wished I could have been in the courtroom to witness the social upheaval. The Queen was so perturbed that she revoked Mother's royal presentation.

In spite of all this, Eric and Granny were both reasonably available as supportive father figures in my early years. They were often playful and clearly clamoring for my loyalty, yet were absent in many ways, too.

It was Granny, of course, who joined us in France soon after Mother and I escaped England (there was little choice but to leave), to evade such turmoil as the trial created. He held the post of father figure. Most sadly, barely a year into our new lives in France, Granny died at sea. We—that is Mother, Granny (my Poppa!) and I—were on the SS *Prinz Ludwig*, voyaging to the Orient. I suspect, now, that it was kind of a celebration that the custody battle was finally over, a way to leave that time of unhappiness behind. Alas, unhappiness was not ours to leave. Granny became ill on the ship. There was not adequate medicine to attack the pneumonia that took him down. I was only six years old, but was still somewhat aware of the drama unfolding.

This commemoration cruise came about barely a year after Mother had disguised me as a small boy in a sailor suit, and the two of us sailed from England to France by camouflage of night. We had exited from the Port of Tilbury and voyaged to Dunkirk, on the appropriately named tug, *Rescue*. I wonder if perhaps the trauma of both Mother and Granny being forced to relinquish all family inheritance and good standing in London society didn't take such an emotional toll on them both, that an exhausted state might have proved literally fatal for Granny.

Be that as it may, after Granny died, I overheard the Captain and Mother in a heated discussion. (I do trust that my memory is sharp enough to recreate the impressive incident.)

"But, Madame. Your husband's dying wish was for burial at sea. It is my duty as the Captain of this ship to uphold that."

"I must insist otherwise, sir. This is too sudden. It would be traumatic for the child! No. I cannot allow this. I take full responsibility for my husband's affairs. No further discussion."

"As you wish, Madame Gordon. As you wish."

At the time I was grateful for Mother's fortitude. The idea of watching the draped body of my beloved Granny slip off board and spiral out of sight into the deep and endless sea haunted me. From my life-lived perspective now, however, it's not such an adverse idea, and I do believe might even be desirable. Nevertheless, Granny's body remained on the ship. The three of us, for the last time as three, disembarked in Colombo, Ceylon, where the burial took place.

I never returned to Ceylon to pay my adult respects to the grave. Had Mother only honored Granny's wish for burial at sea, I might have felt his presence from any shore or spot of land bordering that large and massive body of water. As it was, my bereaved but always stoic mother, widowed now a second time, refused any prolonged ceremony of mourning and remained stalwart. The two of us continued onward, adding an Atlantic crossing for a visit to Chicago, where we visited Mother's sister, Anne Graves. (She was one of the three sisters who made the Prairie Farm expedition. Auntie Anne married Samuel Houghton Graves, one of the Close brothers' partners.)

I remember only fragments of that leg of the journey, for I was young, mourning, and detached. I managed to create an internal safety net to guard against a deep sense of loneliness. I questioned where I belonged, and what a place called home really meant. The tall buildings and city bustle of Chicago were more modern, more American, than London. However, the crowds of people laughing and embracing tugged at my memory and provided momentary flashes of those calm years in England, before the storm of love and divorce changed everything.

Where, then, is the light? I have claimed that to know me, and to appreciate the darkness at the end, you should know some of my early light. Light, too, has multiple interpretations. My light, I'm sure, was in part the coddling I received from Mother, who was always eager to compensate for what she perceived as an unfair upheaval of my childhood. But from my small perspective, my young life was a bright adventure (with the exception of those momentary lapses into dim loneliness), beginning with those lush gardens, toddling about in the company of three black-tongued, tongue-lapping Chows, and making my way through the world with two father figures who doted on me. For those few first years at least, I was kept pretty much unaware of the drama that took place. For this, I must give Mother and her men much credit.

Forgive me if I have kept you too long in this garden of sweet memory. It is time to move on and explain how a (rather) young American woman named Lizzie has become involved with my life in so many serendipitous ways. I, of course, knew nothing about her in my lifetime; she did not arrive on this earth until ten years after my death. Fortunately, we did know firsthand—during each of our lives—two of the same family members: my cousin Margaret, who becomes Lizzie's grandmother, and another cousin, Franklin, in Canada, who later enters this story briefly.

I would like to return to that day when Lizzie first takes earnest notice of me as a child. The year is 1996 and the image of me is almost 100 years old; merely a moment captured; a life journey yet to unfold; a mystery calling to be solved. Who could have known how this one simple collection of cells surrounding and informing and creating this tiny life form called "child" would manifest and enrich and embrace so many other lives? Yes, it is my previous physical self to whom I refer. These newfound connections to family and history and understanding of the world add an entirely new meaning to the life I lived.

Had I known then what I know now, would I have followed the same path? Is this not a question nearly everyone asks at some stage of life, that "what if" path that can never be revealed? Oh yes, what if…? What if…there had been a child? What if…there had been no failure of imagination? What if...what if that pompous personality did not exist?

Ah, and yet. I must consider the directions that those paths might lead. There are not options, for I do not have so much of a choice.

Or perhaps I do, for I eventually choose to leave France, leave my husband, stow away on the Isle of Jersey, and continue west to England, choosing to cross the Channel, despite the risk. Risk is everywhere, hiding in the shadows. Perhaps the reality is a matter of choice about which risks to take. I continue to take risks for the rest of my shortened life, risks I still believe I would embrace over and over again. These risks are what define my life. These risks are the reason that my life has now been revived and brought back into the light of day.

If not for these risks, I believe my life would still be buried in the dark muck and mire of war, lost and forgotten, as so many other lives have been. My risks and choices define this narrative. I regain a voice for myself from the past, added to this collaborative voice from Lizzie with future insight, and together we create this present-day dialogue. It is her voice we must hear now.

*Cecily, my dear.* I am anxious to trust this good fortune. Is it true? Are you at last speaking with me? I've yearned to meet with you for almost one third of my lifetime! I traveled to Paris twice, searching for you. I attended graduate school—at an age older than your age of death at 45—to fulfill my obsession to write about your life. I have consistently sifted through stacks of essays that I composed with you as the subject, multiple drafts of both fiction and nonfiction, based on resourcefulness and historical facts. I persevered with a passion to try and get a handle on how to reach you and honor your story. I audited a course on anti-Semitism as an attempt to understand the historical influence of Nazi Germany and the eventual outcome of your life, and the lives of so many others. I even took a perspectives-in-film class to explore the journey motif through the eyes of a third-generation-removed family chronicler.

In the beginning, I believed I had no right to imagine what anyone who experienced crimes against humanity such as those you witnessed, and experienced first hand, would think or feel. There were so many gaps of information, so many dead ends. But word by word, message by message, and person by person, this quest to bring you to life has become genuine.

The effort has finally paid off. You are present, as real to me as if you were next to me in the flesh. I simply woke up one morning and almost without further consideration (after a decade of puzzling!)

trusted myself enough to know your voice. We began this conversation just as naturally as if we had met for tea.

Together now, let's tell your story. You've made an excellent start. It seems ironic that I waited all these years to hear your voice, and now you're the one introducing my voice. Here we go, then.

# CORRESPONDENCE

Lord Granville Gordon, father of Cecily.
*Mrs. D. Lefort*

*MY DEAR CECILY:* At last, our conversation begins. Today is June 17. Seventy-three years ago today, Petain surrendered France to Germany. Seventy years ago on this very date you dropped back into France as a spy. This is also your wedding anniversary. It seems a good time to begin.

I have discovered artifacts about your life that you did not know existed, due to the war and the lack of sufficient room for you and your husband to understand each other. I know what became of Alix after you died and the war ended. The future is good and life-affirming. But had you lived on, what would have become of your marriage? I feel that the loss of your husband as a companion in your life might have been too large to bear. Sadly, you did have a notion as to the extent of his affection just before you died.

As it is, there are many beautiful people who have been born through the lineage of Alix and the woman he married after the war. Is this a good thing, then? I could of course write a happy ending for you, but I fear that's not the direction we're heading. The more closely I come to know you, the more my concern for you gains momentum. I have witnessed the dark places from black and white photographs in history books. I have walked the land of Theresienstadt. I have persisted through evidence at Ravensbrück Memorial in Paris. I cannot stop this feeling of foreboding.

Already, the finale looms on the horizon.

*Dear Lizzie:* Yes, yes! *Mais s'il vous plâit,* slow down! I introduced a sense of urgency, I know, though I'm feeling more balanced now that you've joined me. We must give ourselves time to digest and assimilate. I insist. Now, please....

*Dear Cecily:* I will momentarily close my eyes to your future. Let's find a beginning point for this journey and travel it together. I will start with that time in America when your mother and her two sisters lived among the Gentlemen Farmers. As you described, their brother Edward preceded the sisters' arrival in Iowa. I am eager to tell you that this man, your Uncle Teddy, is my great grandfather, Grad. He remained in America, married, and named one of his daughters Margaret, the second Margaret in this family tree. She is my Grammie, and your cousin. When your mother, Margaret, returned to England, your Aunt Annie remained in America for a short time, before moving to Paris. As I have come to discover, Annie—affectionately called Kitty by family—became your lifeline during the consuming years of war. The third Humble sister, your Aunt Susan, married Frederic Close's brother, William. For a while they lived in Chicago, but eventually they too returned to England. They had children, and their children had children.

One of the miracles of time, and our modern day technology, is how we can trace the intersection of lives through generations. So it is that I was able to locate and contact one of Susan and William Close's grandsons, James B. Close. He was in his 80s by the time I wrote this letter to him. It is dated February 7, 2002. A leap, to be sure, but that is an example of how I became caught in the webs that weave our journeys together.

> *Dear Mr. James B. Close,*
>
> *I come down through the Humble family line. I have a photograph of Mom and Dad when they visited you back in 1987. They are standing by the cannon on your estate in Surrey. I am charmed with what you wrote on the back of the photo: "The cannons shot off for the wedding of Fergie and Andrew. It made such a splendid noise for all to hear and knocked the apples out of the tree."*
>
> *I am very interested in knowing more about Cecily Close and her mother, Margaret. I am particularly interested in Cecily's life in France during WWII, and her death for helping the English pilots. Can you be of any help? I understand that Cecily's mother, Margaret, has quite a history, too. Can you share any of that?*
> *With warm regards,*
> *Elizabeth*

February 13, 2002 reply from James:
*Dear Elizabeth,*

> *We were delighted to get your letter. The Humble family is of course related to the Closes! My grandmother, Susan Humble, was not only beautiful, but charming.*

*Then there was "Great Aunt" Betty who married Houghton Graves and lived in luxury in Paris. She scared me stiff! Then we come to Margaret. She married Fred Close, who we suppose was the brightest of the four Close brothers connected with Iowa. Fred died playing polo in Des Moines, leaving Margaret a widow. But no languishing widow was she, she "took off," and her behavior was much disapproved of by the whole family. Then came the famous trial, and Margaret's flight with her daughter to France. This daughter, Cecily, married a French doctor, Lefort. As we all know, she died in the hands of the Germans, consequent on her courageous activities in the Résistance.*

*There is little we know of about the history of that family after the flight to France, no doubt bad feelings prevented much contact.*

*I expect you know all this anyway.*

*With our best wishes,*

*James*

*Dear Cecily:* Of course, you have by now beautifully rendered that time of your mother's life. When Jimmy answered my first letter (we became quite familiar through our years of conversation) he assumed I already knew "all this."

"But I don't know any of this!" I shouted into the day.

What was most important in Jimmy's explanation is that your name had become Lefort, a name no one in my family had talked about before. This provided a key starting point, which eventually became the final point.

At first, I wanted to know about your life just before the war. My meander into your childhood began later, when I too realized that, to appreciate the dark, I had to know who you were as a child, and of course how your mother's colorful life influenced you.

Point to consider: you married Dr. Alix Lefort. Being the romantic that I am, I first imagined the scene when you and Alix parted, in the turmoil and angst of the German invasion. There is also another subtle detail that I am curious if you will notice. Allow me to tell my version.

June 1940, France. It's been said that even the birds left Paris when the Nazis invaded, and fields of lavender in southern France lost their dusky hue to the gunmetal air. Coastal waters off Brittany churned with the turbulence of boats in exodus, and angst unraveled a couple's embrace.

Night took forever to arrive, yet consumed the sky too quickly. Though married sixteen years that same week and no longer young, Dr. Alix Lefort and his wife clung to each other like new lovers. Germans now occupied Paris and an as yet little-known General named de Gaulle had put out a call for French citizens to resist the unacceptable surrender. Perhaps Doctor and Cicely Lefort heard the plea while dining in their flat in Paris overlooking Boulevard Bosquet, before the songbirds disappeared. They might have joined friends at Ladurée, drawn together with defiance and hope. The landmark Eiffel, swastikas flying, confirmed that invasion was no longer impossible. The pounding of the sound of this impossibility reverberated across cobblestoned passageways. Panic set in, an urgency to take leave. No one knew for how long, no one knew to what future, no one knew what would become of their past.

Having fled Paris, the doctor and his wife headed west with the wave of the invasion instead of joining the southern march of their exiled comrades, keeping momentum until they anxiously arrived at their second home, a scrubbed Brittany stone villa in St. Cast. The impending departure was unavoidable, for the occupation left little choice but for Cicely to escape to her native England (where she would again be referred to as Cecily, and not the French version, Cicely, that Alix called his wife).

A hasty return to St. Cast propelled Alix and Cicely toward another urgent drive to the port of St. Malo for the final departure. The docks seethed with activity as panicked British citizens crowded onto distressed fishing boats. Here we find the doctor and his wife, stalwart against the darkness of night and coastal winds battering the moored ships that lurched at the end of their cables like tethered beasts eager to set themselves free.

Gone, for Alix and Cicely, are the glorious days of sailing peaceful waters off their private beach below the St. Cast villa. Ahead loom the ominous waters opening to the Channel filled with German U-boats. The unknown lies dead center ahead and the time for them to part had arrived.

L: Well, Cecily. How did I do?

CL: Almost spot on, dear Lizzie. Except, well, we weren't exactly "like new lovers" anymore, though there was an intense longing to hold on, to have our lives return to the comfortable way we had been for so long. And, to be true, our marriage had conflict, as any marriage does, but for us, there were underlying tensions that this invasion and war allowed us to avoid confronting. Indeed, I fully expected to remain on Jersey for a while and then return to Alix in France and confront our differences. Little did we know that the world and our lives were to become as tumultuous as the sea was that night of my exodus.

I am also impressed with your subtle, and I presume conditional, switch in the spelling of my name, from the English version of Cecily, to my French adaptation, Cicely, as dear Alix would have spoken. I did often have conflict with which version to use on identification papers, being of course first British, but then for the greater portion of my life living and marrying in France where I was identified as Cicely. Bravo, Lizzie. Perhaps for the sake of clarity, from here on out we shall impose the French adaptation. *D'accord?*

I must ask though, in that first letter you wrote to James B. Close, who are Fergie and Andrew?

L: Well thank you, dear, for your generous praise. The recognition of cultural differences in the spelling of your name has provided a bit of confusion, even within family records. Since my first knowledge of you, I have called you Cecily. However, from this moment on, for the purpose of this journey, you shall own your French version and be Cicely. *Vraiment.*

Ah, yes. Let's see, Prince Andrew is one of Queen Elizabeth's children, and he married a woman named.... Wait, Elizabeth wasn't Queen until 1952, so you would have known her as the eldest daughter of your King George VI. Indeed, later in this story, Alix petitions the King to recognize your valor, and the King does.

CL: Perhaps we're getting ahead of ourselves, but thank you for providing this context. It is important for me to remember. It rather sounds as if the royal family has stories to tell as well.

L: Now comes the question every couple gets asked at some point. How did you and Alix meet?

CL: You will recall that Granny died quite unexpectedly after Mother and I moved to France. I suppose I always missed having a male figure in my life, and I suspect that one of my attractions to Alix was his maturity. Though he was only ten years older than I, his demeanor was a wonderful mix of gentleman and protector. Of course, he was French, which added a lovely romantic air. Also, it was an earlier time, the First World War, a time of political crisis when unlikely relationships had the opportunity to seal. (Ah, yes, I recognize the significance of this as foreshadowing in both of our futures.) Nonetheless, I was, at the age of nineteen, working as a nurse's aid, taking care of a French doctor suffering from tuberculosis toward the ending of that war. Perhaps our common ground of caring for the wounded was a source of familiarity. Mother had recently died, and this French doctor—yes, it is Alix!— became the closest thing I related to as family.

L: Aha! That is a bit what I suspected as well. May I take such liberty to have a go with how I pictured your courtship?

CL: Oh, yes dear, by all means. Already, as I am coming to know you, I imagine you will have added a layer of romance on top of the truth; but I find this trait charming, dear Lizzie. And shall I say, hopefully not inappropriately for what circles around a very dark time, but right now anyway, I so very much enjoy your stories. Please, continue.

1920s, France. Dr. Alix Lefort had finally met a woman who shared his passion for life and the sea. Already Dr. Lefort owned a sailboat, named *L'Ariane*. Would Cicely have known the history of the 1812 French frigate christened *L'Ariane*, rigged with 44 guns and run aground where it caught fire and exploded, which so inspired the christening of the doctor's own boat? Chances are more likely that Alix impressed the young lady by showing her his portfolio of aquatints memorializing French ships. Plausibly, a collection of paintings would be displayed on the Brittany stone walls of the doctor's villa on the coast of St. Cast.

Imagine Cicely, a sensitive and vulnerable woman, already having lived a life of drama, now more or less on her own, heading into the possibility of a life of security mixed with adventure alongside this distinguished gentleman. Beneath the villa stretched the couple's own private beach. Across the waters, the string of Channel Islands awaited their habitual landings.

Say you are young, pretty, and mostly brave. Already you are alone in your immediate world; already you have witnessed the effects of war, tended to the wounded, learned that not all wounds mend, that not all soldiers return home. You are whisked away from the bustle of Paris toward the pull of the tides. Late afternoon sea mist greets your arrival and in the distance, the low, deep yawn of a fog horn. You wear appropriately casual shoes and trousers. The doctor leads you over the stone threshold, through a framed set of white French doors beneath a view-spanning window two stories up where you will look over your shoulder toward the sea and view the stretch of vacant beach that peeks through the hydrangea hedge. The aroma of roses that followed you up the path still hangs in the muted air. Deep vines grip the stone facade.

A fire has been laid by Anna, the caretaker, knowing Doctor is arriving with a lady friend. One night, at least, will be spent in this villa overlooking the sea. Likely two or more, for this first time, anyway. Days filled with brackish air, as familiar to you as your own skin. The excitement of those first few hours when a shared passion for sailing is realized. And by night, hunger and thirst—perhaps for more than the food and wine at the table—will no doubt linger.

Still, a genteel respect prevails, and this first visit, the first of a lifetime of sojourns to the house above the sea, will remain the foundation of commitment to follow. So the lovebirds return to the cosmopolitan culture of Paris, where the resolute man and the impressionable woman must for the sake of appearances maintain separate residences, though the path between is traveled more and more frequently.

CL (chuckling): As I suspected: romantic! I do beg to differ though, that having survived my childhood turmoil, the death of both my parents, and already one world war, I was more callous than vulnerable, though I can see how a modern day American such as yourself would have trouble knowing this. You are correct, though, about Alix's propriety, and thank you for mentioning Anna. She was such a dear. I do miss her still. She did tease us so and was frightfully clever about pushing us gently toward becoming a couple.

However—oh my, how should I go about explaining this without deflating your bubble? Your adaptation of that lovely scene for a couple at the launch of a relationship is something I would like to embrace, would that it were true. In reality, our blessed St. Cast *maison* was not realized for another eight years following our marital union. Indeed, though I fear this may sound arrogant, it was my family inheritance that allowed us to purchase the land and build our seaside villa. Suddenly I realize how this reflects Grandmama's investment in her prairie land all those years ago as well; another family tradition, perhaps. I loved how *les jardins* that flowed from along the stone façade upon the overview to the beach below were endearingly designed to remind me of the English gardens of my childhood. Yes, the same as in the photographs that so drew you to me. We christened the parcel *la hune* to honor the top of the land we claimed, and echo the sails of the yachts we already revered.

Good lord, how did you know about L'Ariane? Or Anna, for that matter? But first, let me take a turn in this passage! I would like to tell you, now, a little about what was going on in Paris in the 20s. What a time it was to be young, in love—yes, we were in love—and in Paris.

Our lovely city was at full swing in rebound following the war. Paris was brimming with energy for all things new. The pulse of jazz rippled up and down the boulevard of Montmartre. We humorously witnessed the influx of expatriate artists. My conservative Alix could barely contain an outburst of laughter when these Americans literally tripped over easels, knocking portraits-in-progress to the cobblestones; their romantic heads were *en état d'ébriété* from our fine French liqueurs and wreathed in clouds of smoke.

I was emboldened to have my curls cut short, as was the style, and even braved a conservatively shorter hemline. Alix was at first aghast, but finally warmed to my youthful experimentation. Women were all too delighted to surrender the constricting design of a corset, as we nurses had already achieved, for practicality's sake, during the war.

Having broadened his views, Alix—himself a conundrum of romantic and playful characteristics, mixed with the conservative—complimented me. He confessed that my silhouette could carry the prevailing corset-less avant-garde fashion well, in spite of the "aristocratic edge" as he liked to tease, that came out of my British heritage. Oh my, what a mix of contradictions I was for the dear man.

My mother's tendency to break the rules, yet with a proper air, weighed on my own sense of self in conflicting ways. Add to this my rather free-spirited French upbringing, to say nothing of the influence of my travels to America. I was a mix of cultures and messages, young and impetuous, on the arm of a man of medicine. A French doctor! Nevertheless, it would have been unreasonable to expect our softer sides not to succumb to the times. So we joined the throngs sauntering past studio windows filled with spotlighted Man Ray nudes (surely I blushed). I was quite fond of American jazz and I so dearly remember one warm evening stroll when we heard Coleman Hawkins' *I'm Gonna See You* wafting from a corner café. Alix insisted that we take an outdoor table and enjoy an aperitif. How could Paris have been anything but consuming?

L: Seems like such an exciting time to be alive, and to be *so* alive. I have always been drawn to what I naïvely (and romantically) imagined the 1940s were like during that time of war. Of course someone like myself who has no real idea of just what "war" embraces, can easily take the passionate view. But your description here, just after the First World War, is much how I pictured such a time, with the celebration of life going on, knowing how fragile the world really was. Now, speaking of playful and romantic French men, I would also like to introduce you to another person who has been vital to my recovering your life. I will reference my travel chronicle to recreate the scene.

It is the summer of 2002. A trip to France in July with my mother, my sister, and her daughter, increases my awareness of the history of the Second World War and the Résistance in Paris. Here we are, three generations of American women, dressed in a mix of silk, linen, and muslin, not at all sure what to expect of this exhibit within the *Hôtel National des Invalides*. As we walk through the *Musée de la Libération*, it is difficult for me to concentrate on the photographs of exploitation and starvation of prisoners that are displayed in a section focused on Ravensbrück, one of the German Concentration Camps. I was beginning to learn of the intentions for this labor camp, to contain mostly women, political prisoners, and those creative human beings who associated outside society's mainstream. In the dim light and with the hour of closing upon us, I cannot read the names embroidered on a framed scarf by a group of women who were in the camp in 1944, but I know it is possible that Cicely's hands once held the fabric.

I search book stalls along the Seine for World War II memorabilia and buy a document published in 1944 titled *Women in the War, Volume II*. It is browned and crisp with age and feels as if it might disintegrate inside the plastic wrapping. A collection of black and white photographs of life in Paris in the 1940s, the unexpected crossing of the wide wooden-planked pedestrian bridge with a commemoration by General de Gaulle to the comrades in the cause of Résistance, and the Ministry of Defense Memorial to Liberation that we find underground off the point of Notre Dame, all confirm my need to return another year and research Cicely's life.

L: You see, Cicely, the information in the letters I received from James B. Close that previous spring had already created a desire to discover as much as possible about your life as a spy. While we were in France, we stayed with family friends who live near Avignon, Madeleine and René Jamois. This René turned out to be my most diligent researcher. As soon as we returned to America, I sent a letter to him, explaining my interest in your life and history of the invasion of France.

> *Dear René,*
>
> *I didn't take the time to talk to you about a large interest of mine. I believe I was too overwhelmed with ideas about this project when we saw you to approach the subject then. I will tell you now, and if you know any contacts or think of anything, please send it my way. Our relative, Cicely Lefort, was part of the French Résistance in the early 1940s. She was a courier in S.E. France and was captured near Montélimar. From there she ended up at Ravensbrück, where she died in 1945. If you know of any information that would enlighten my search, I'd appreciate the contact.*

L: When we visited the Jamoises in their home in Le Pontet that summer, René had reminisced about the day in 1945 when France was liberated by the Americans. As a boy of 17, he adopted a lasting impression and dedication to the United States in spite of international transgressions over the years. From this point on, Cicely, René dedicated himself to finding what he could about your life. So began our many years of transcontinental correspondence and amazing discoveries.

CL: Oh my, dear Lizzie. Already I'm remembering that area of southern France so very well. Of course that was where I spent most of my time, short though it was, as a courier. And you do realize, by now I'm sure, that I was recruited by Special Operation Executives (SOE) as a British agent, even though we did indeed support and work with the French Résistance.

And another point I should mention: we were actually identified as agents, secret agents if you like that drama, but not literally spies. *D'accord*?

L: Your point about agent and not spy is well taken. I feel only a wee bit bruised. Yes, I say that with admiration, you do know! Yet it's true that the idea of "spy" holds more drama than "agent." I have learned, as well, that the label of "spy" was imposed on secret agents by the Germans so they could execute the prisoners of war whom they identified as spies. By that, I mean the consequence of wearing the colored triangle prisoners were assigned that designated their "crime." Your triangle as a political prisoner was red, as you are well aware. After the war—yes, dear, later there will be much involving "after" that we will address in this conversation—a British judgment was proclaimed clarifying this distinction, allowing that by the Geneva Convention, secret agents were not spies and it was a crime to execute them.

Be that as it may, I dare say that as we continue, the word "spy" will crop up equivalent, for this story, with "secret agent." Will you accept this, my dear secret agent spy?

CL: You are not to worry. I understand this distinction and approve. Now, back to your visit to France. I am intrigued. You must have passed right near Lyon, and Montélimar, yes? But I don't want to think about that just yet. Tell me more about this man, this René. To think he was but a boy when the world was at war and this middle aged lady was scurrying through hedgerows, steadfastly committed to a cause of peace and kindness. René is now talking with you. It is dreamlike (all things being relative, of course).

L: Yes, we did go past those towns, and I did indeed look out the window of the TGV train (so fast!) and try to imagine you out there, perhaps on a rickety bicycle or in the back of a lorry. And here, wait, let me go get something, just here in this bookshelf. Let me see, ah, there: *Truffe au Nougat*, the box I purchased during this excursion. It held a number of exquisite truffles, the kind that have been made in Montélimar since 1837. The box still has the delicate gold string that was wrapped around it, with the sweetest small twisted silver charm dangling from it. Yes, I know it's wise to realize that those nougats were not something you had any time to enjoy during your intense travels through Montélimar.

CL: That's all lovely. I am mesmerized, imagining the world you now live in, and fascinated by this search for my life that has so taken over your attention. I even wonder what an adventure the two of us might have had, would that our lives intersected in some common "real" time. At least we have this time now to share. So pray, do continue with this man, René Jamois. *S'il vous plaît.*

L: But of course. My correspondence with both René and Jimmy consisted only of the old fashioned handwritten letters sent through what we now call "snail mail." Of course, our slow process of mail is nothing compared to the war pace through Red Cross. The lapse of time during the war becomes most significant in the direction your relationship with Alix took, creating misunderstandings beyond either of your control, and of which neither of you were aware. But we'll get to that. Regardless, it wasn't until the next summer that René's lucid accounts of discovery began to arrive. Let's go to that day, July 11, 2003, when I received a package from René.

One of the first decoratively postmarked envelopes arrives at my door. It contains news from René: he sent a notice to the monthly *Le Patriote résistant* in search of information about the Résistance network in southeast France where Cicely was an agent. Through this published notice he received a letter from a Madame Dumont, living in Provence. Though she did not ever meet Cicely—she, too, was 17 when Paris was liberated—she volunteered her time to join our search. René received a second letter as a result of the notice, from a Madame Postel-Vinay, that included a copy of a sketch of Cicely drawn by France Audoul, an artist who was in the same railcar as Cicely on the way to Ravensbrück. "We never knew how this young lady died," wrote Madame Postel-Vinay.

CL: Excuse me, we must stop a moment. Madame Postel-Vinay? Someone who knew me back then has written to your René now? But who is she, this Postel-Vinay? Of course, that name would most likely have come to her after the war. She refers to me as "young lady?" My goodness. I was nearly 45 years old, one of the older agents, if not the oldest! Ah, but she remembered me from Ravensbrück, where perhaps at 45 I did seem a young lady, vulnerable anyway, in my poor health and sorry state. But who wasn't in a sorry state by then! And Postel-

Vinay may have worked with the Résistance, not SOE. It's kind of falling into place now. Be patient with me, dear Lizzie! This is all so much for me to take in. This talking opens up all sorts of memories and confusions. I'm frightened, but also intrigued to continue.

L: I'm sorry, Cicely. I know this must be hard, for you do have an idea of how the story unfolds. But one day at a time, one memory, one person, yes? Madame Postel-Vinay's given name is Anise. Does that ring a bell?

CL: Her name *is...*? She is still alive? Even now?

L: I believe so. We know of course that she was alive back in 2003 when she wrote to René. Anise knew you well enough to remember you almost 60 years later. Ah yes, and in that context, I see why she referred to you as a young woman. My, how time alters our perspective! Anise was only 20 when she joined the Résistance, so she would have been about 78 years when she wrote to René, and since you—you died so long ago, you are to her frozen at the age of 45 when she knew you. She remembers you not as her 21-year-old and your 45-year-old prisoner of war ages, but as a woman of 78, looking back at a "young lady." You must have left quite a fond impression with those whose lives you touched, Cicely.

I remember now, too, why I know of Anise in connection with you. Also in 2003 a documentary film was released called *Sisters in Resistance*. The film tells the stories of four women, all Gentiles, who joined the resistance movement in France after the German invasion in 1940. Anise was one of the four women interviewed by film Director Maia Wechsler. Besides Anise, there was Geneviève de Gaulle, Germaine Tillion, and Jacqueline Péry. I watched this film with fascination, as I was already aware that your life had crossed the path of at least two of these women, Anise and Geneviève.

CL: Yes, Geneviève! I remember—but this is just too much at once. I must rest. Please, you do the talking for a while. I promise I will join back in.

L: Anise and Germaine Tillion met on the train to Ravensbrück. Again, I am struck by the impact of perspective. If we take those words in abstract, it could sound like such a lovely adventure "on the train to...." But of course, put them in their context, and an entirely different picture is conjured. You and Geneviève were on a train, let's label it "transport," a couple weeks later. It was identified in documents as the 27000 train. You all arrived at Ravensbrück in February of 1944. Geneviève passed through the dehumanizing indoctrination process before you.

The prisoner number inked on your wrist (27.962) was only 600 digits after Geneviève's (27.372). That may seem like a great distance, but considering the thousands of women who passed through the line-up, they were relatively close. You were in the same block as Germaine, and I believe also with Corrie Ten Boom, who arrived at the camp a few months after your transport.

It's quite possible you would remember Corrie. You might even have been a source of information to help her adjust to this frightful milieu and survive as long as she managed. Yes, she did survive, and wrote her story about the war, a book most of the world now is familiar with, titled *The Hiding Place*. Each of the four *Sisters in Resistance* also published memoirs: Jacqueline, *Surviving Ravensbrück*; Geneviève, *The Dawn of Hope: A Memoir of Ravensbrück*; Germaine, *Ravensbrück*; and Anise, simply *Life*.

(For most survivors who finally shared their stories, nearly the rest of their lives had to pass before they could reflect about their experiences and memories. And in your case, dear Cicely, long after your life on earth has passed, you and I are writing yours. Give some thought, if you would, to what we should title your story. Something light and airy, perhaps, to brighten the shadow?)

Corrie was a few years older than you at the time, so this might have created a bond. Or perhaps you encountered Betsie, Corrie's older sister, who also was at Ravensbrück. Perhaps Corrie recounted tales about her brother, Willem, who she distinctly claims "saw things." Even in 1927, Willem wrote about "a terrible evil that was taking root in Germany. Seeds of contempt for human life were being planted, such as the world had never seen." Corrie wrote that people laughed at Willem for his ideas, but it did come to pass.

Once at the camp (yes, again, "camp" as if it were a resting spot on an outing), Geneviève was reunited with Jacqueline Péry, a compatriot in the Résistance in Paris. They later confessed that the nightmare of their experiences led to the joy of their friendship, grounded by their depth of compassion and love for each other, a level of strength they would not have had otherwise. Germaine declared, "If I survived, I owe the fact first to chance, then to anger—the desire one day to reveal these crimes—and finally to a set of friendships."

This is all beginning to sound so detached, Cicely. I'm spilling out names as if I'm making a list for a dinner party. Forgive me. You must know I don't intend it to come off this way. I want to get the facts right, to make sense of all this. To at least help you see the whole picture through all these windows that you couldn't even conceive of at the time. There's just so much to understand and discover, for both of us!

CL: They all survived? Can this be true?

L: Yes, these women survived! And because those women (and many more) survived, you too survived. How so? Why look, dear Cicely, Anise still remembers you, from whatever brief time in passing you both shared in 1943 in the dismal and inhumane condition of one of the now historic concentration camps. (Though rumors persisted, no one in the world at the time could believe such so-called "lies.")

Each person who survived represents the power of the human spirit. Evil did not win. These women—Anise, Germaine, Geneviève, Jacqueline, and Corrie—continued their lives. They went out into the world to tell their stories, to remember those whose earthly lives were taken, to begin worldwide humanitarian projects, to be witness to the beauty of this world that the hand of self-righteousness could not kill. These women were alive on my television screen (good lord, you don't even "know" television!) when I sat in my living room in America and watched the film about their lives in Europe. We are all, in some extraordinary ways, connected.

CL: Tell me again, this Germaine Tillion. Something is coming back to me. Tillion.... Oh dear. Emilie! Of course, Emilie Tillion, Germaine's mother! Oh yes, yes, my goodness. I do remember. I do. And she, Lizzie? Did she...?

L: I had forgotten this too! Oh my, please, I must find this paper. Here it is...ah yes. Going back to Anise, of course, and her letter to René that included that sketch of you, and one of Emilie. Yes, here, look. Remember? The artist France Andoul was on the same railway freight car as you were, on the way to the Ravensbrück. Andoul made many sketches of life in the camp. Right here is the sketch of you, and one of Emilie, and one of Evelyne Arnel, identified as secretary of the Résistance movement.

CL: Oh my. Lizzie. Such sadness, but also such light still captured in our faces here. A testament to beauty from within, and of Andoul's talent, if I dare say. But dear me, beneath each of our sketches, there, and there, and there, the words MORTE A RAVENSBRÜCK. So, Emilie too. I'm exhausted.

L: I feel exhausted now, too. I'm going to translate from my travel chronicle, with notes I have added from my research, for I do not have the energy to present this to you in conversation. So now, this time, we move up to late winter, 2007. Hold on, dear Cicely. This part will reveal more about Alix's life, and marriage, after the war. I'm sorry. From this point on, there may not be much of a break; it cannot be avoided.

While all these years I thought that finding any information about Dr. Lefort might be the last hope to learn more about Cicely — I had searched and found one Alix Lefort among a long list of Leforts in the Paris phone book during my previous journey in 2002 — I have no success.

Then one day a letter from René announces that Mme Dumont *(note to Cicely: Remember, Mme Dumont contacted René for the same posting that Anise responded to back in 2003, so you see, these communications went on for years, discovering you!)* has not only discovered that Cicely's husband, Dr. Lefort, survived the war, but she has remarkably found the woman he married after the war. Mme Lefort still lives in France and, like most of my primary contacts, she is in her late 80s. It will be through this prodigious woman and her family of daughters that the story of Cicely rises, almost literally, from the ashes.

But first, a return to Paris in the 20s, and the union of Dr. Lefort and Cicely.

# PRE-WAR PARIS

Marriage of Cicely Gordon and Dr. Alix Lefort.
*Lefort family collection*

**L: CICELY? ARE YOU OKAY** with this? Shall I continue? All right, then. Here we go.

On June 17, 1924, Ernest Alix Lefort and Cicely Margot Gordon signed their names for the last time as single adults. The wedding took place in a Parisian Catholic church with twin guards dressed in Napoleonic style regalia, complete with plume tipped tricorne helmets, broadswords, and substantial silver-capped staffs. The groom wore a six-button vest and classic tailcoat, and in the crook of his arm rested a top hat. A less-flamboyant cravat rather than a bow tie was naturally nonnegotiable. The right hand holding the balanced top hat also clutched that hand's discarded glove, the cloth fingers trailing up the side of the brim like magical rabbit ears.

The bride was stunning in a simple yet elegant ivory gown, pulled in by a ribbon-like band about her narrow hips, stylishly shortened to reveal her trim ankles. Across her elbow-length gloved arm she carried a span of white calla lilies and simple greens, wrapped with a linen handkerchief. Her lips turned up contentedly, though she surely felt the void of her mother at this astounding event.

Together the couple walked from the subdued coolness of the church along a floral carpet and out into the June-inspired day, the ink of their signatures still damp, the promise to love, to protect, and to cherish, still resounding in the air.

CL: I must say that you do a wonderful job of recreating the lovely event, Lizzie; such a relief in the midst of such a discouraging war narrative, dear. I'm feeling better. You observed all that in the one wedding photograph of Alix and me? Fine, indeed. Thank you for the transcription. Please continue with your travel notes buoyed by research. It is, quite frankly, a pleasure to let you take the lead here, and to have a break in the conversation. Your records hit the mark. Those times before the war are such a joy to relive, in spite of, well, the final outcome. Yet as you point out, all was not lost. Lives did thrive, and eventually more came to exist, as a consequence of wartime upheavals. I am just now beginning to realize this, and even embrace their futures.

This is when I would so enjoy a nice cup of tea, were that possible.

L: And I, wishing to please you, would ask, "one lump, or two?" Place yourself in that comforting scene and allow me to describe how I imagine your lives to have been following your marriage, during those years in Paris before war once again ripped the world apart. I think I've got it pretty close to the way things were. You be the judge.

The next fifteen years in the lives of the bride and groom become hazy, with muted colors and soft edges, much like Marc Chagall's painting, *Solitude*—his response to anti-Semitic energies in the world of 1933. History reveals events that no doubt influence Doctor and Madame Lefort. Across the world, countries forge ahead through uprisings and rumors.

Ernest Hemingway meets F. Scott Fitzgerald for the first time at Dingo Bar in Paris. Literary circles become critics of a society symbolized by the "lost generation," often meeting at an American bookshop that Sylvia Beach created, called Shakespeare and Company. Charles Lindbergh flies solo from New York to France, and a headline that reads "Lindy Hops the Atlantic" inspires the Lindy Hop in an up-and-coming jazz scene. Construction of the Empire State Building begins, and the New York Stock Exchange heads toward "Black Thursday."

Europe continues to struggle with post-war reparations. Mussolini gains Fascist power in Italy while Germany heads toward economic and moral depression, increasing the political propaganda appeal of a zealot named Adolph Hitler. For a significant time, Hitler incredibly comes to represent a reasonable alternative to what the people see as chaos and decline. His earlier Beer Hall Push arrest and imprisonment give him 14 months of nothing but time on his hands to rant, resulting in his political diatribe, *Mein Kampf* (*My Struggle*), which soon becomes the militant minority's Nazi Party platform. Translations of this inflammatory political manifesto into English or French are *verboten*, even though the world at large would scorn at the possibility of Nazi domination.

Doctor and Madame Lefort build a personal history during their time spent together between their flat in Paris and their villa, *La Hune*, near the fishing village of St Cast. The little beach below the villa becomes their playground, a beach that later plays a part in Cicely's war years. By the mid-1930s, rumblings of upheaval take root when German troops march into the Rhineland, threatening the borders based on the Treaty of Versailles.

But in spite of the peril of yet another war, the couple can still enjoy the best *La Ville-lumière* has to offer—swaths of lavender, earthy Bordeaux, aromatic Roquefort cheese and decadent Crème Brûlée dining at *Café-A l'Ami Pierrot*, with the constant din of ragtime floating through doors and windows still kept safely opened.

Doctor and Madame of course avoid going near the Moulin Rouge, a popular entertainment destination for German troops frequented by Paris songbirds such as the legendary cabaret singer, Édith Piaf, known in France as *La Môme Piaf*, or The Little Sparrow. In Paris, the couple enjoy the choice between the still new sound-cinema where Cicely can swoon over Jean Gabin in *La Grande Illusion*, or the exotic world of the *Théâtre des Champs-Elysées*, where Alix might admire the antics of the singer Josephine Baker, an American expatriate who will later also join the world of spies, hiding coded messages between the pages of her sheet music.

During this prelude to war, another American citizen who chooses to live abroad is keeping notes. William Shirer has what some might describe as a crystal ball; not one that literally sees the future, but certainly a perspective, bordering on premonition, from both inside and outside at the same time. He intermingles travel across Europe with observations from Berlin to report a unique interpretation of the war-torn world. On April 20, 1937, Hitler's 51st birthday, Shirer records that the military attachés of many countries, including France and the United States, seem impressed by Hitler's two-hour salute as the German artillery marches past the Institute of Technology. The world is not able to comprehend how the "feverish efforts" of the Third Reich are forcing an exclusive agenda to manipulate the masses.

Perhaps not ready to accept the impossibility of facing war again, Doctor takes his wife on a cruise. Love of the sea and salt air in their blood provide solace in a world turning in on itself. Although the ship *Queen Mary* embarks amid fanfare on her maiden voyage across the Atlantic, Doctor and Madame Lefort choose not to take the cruise to

America. Having logged countless hours on their sailboat off the northern coast of Brittany, they instead head south where they board a ship destined for Syria. It could be that Cicely is a fan of Agatha Christie's very popular mystery novels, and most probably the intrigue of *Death on the Nile* has taken over where the fairy tales have been forgotten.

A cruise for two on the Mediterranean holds the allure of romance, the treasures of ancient civilizations, the promise of mystery— just the right draw for an established middle-aged couple wishing to hold on to waning dreams of propagation and peace on the horizon. Somewhere along the journey, perhaps seated together at the Captain's table one night, Alix and Cicely meet another adventure-seeking duo from France, Monsieur and Mme Pouget. By the time both couples return home and empty the desert sand and broken seashells from their luggage, a lasting friendship has formed. At some point after their return to Paris, surely a reunion is planned, perhaps at the Pouget home. It could be during this initial gathering that Alix and Cicely are introduced to the Pouget's teenage daughter, Janine. The perspective on their lives does not allow clarity from this distance, and there is no possible clue for these families to know then how this daughter will come to enter the story of the Leforts in a remarkable way.

Meanwhile, in the south of France, another London-born adventurer makes the most of sailing her family's yacht. Diana Hope Rowden, fifteen years younger than Cicely, will join her path when they later both enlist in the Women's Auxiliary Air Force (WAAF) in 1941, and Special Operations Executives (SOE) two years later. The common threads of England, France, and the sea, as well as timely recruitment, will one day draw them into each other's circles.

Yet a third enterprising woman, Noor-Un-Nisa Inayat Khan, will enter Cicely's sphere during wartime. Born in the Kremlin, Moscow, and the same age as Diana Rowden, Noor moves with her American mother and Indian father to Paris. There she studies languages and child psychology and writes fairy tales that are published and broadcast. Perhaps Cicely found magic listening to those children's tales coming from a sound box while she curled by the fire, dreaming of the day she might bear a child of her own. But after ten

years of marriage without conception, the couple must finally accept
that the likelihood of children is not in their future, and the lure of
fairy tales will be gone by the wayside. As yet another world war
becomes likely, the paths of these three childless women head toward
mutual adventure and eventual destruction.

CL: Dear Lizzie. You have done your research. My admiration
grows. I dare say that Alix would also have been taken in with your
investigative energy. It might be fair to say that perhaps you too
inherited a bit of our Humble family's ability to "spy" and take on a
great adventure. I'm smiling as I say that, Lizzie. You are charming.
And I see that I've regained some energy after envisioning that
lovely pot of tea. Now, would you care to hear a few amendments to
your interpretation, no criticism intended? Yes? *D'accord.*

We were quite aware of that cultural energy you mention. Alix
kept up with the news diligently. As it was often just the two of us,
and Anna and Alix's mother of course when we went to La Hune, it
seemed there was a constant flow of intellectual conversation
between us. I suppose because we had lived through the first war,
any hint of political turmoil was taken seriously. As we headed
deeper into the late 30s the Paris cafés, as you suggest, practically
throbbed with lively posturing. Alix never tired of the discussions,
but I began to withdraw from the angst I felt was beginning to
wheedle into our peaceful lives, as the injustices toward our fellow
Parisians were beginning to surface.

At this moment, my dear, I must digress and insist, yes I insist!
that you allow me to insert a bit of my history at this opportune
occasion: Édith Piaf! She was just being recognized as a rising star. I
suppose that Alix and I would not have been much aware of her
lovely, enticing voice, were it not for another fascinating bit of
knowledge I acquired. For you see, dear Lizzie, she was named after
a British nurse and war heroine from the Great War, Edith Cavell.
How do I know this? Listen and I will tell.

It is fair to say that my enlistment in the nursing corps in the
Great War was in a large part due to the inspiration of Ms. Cavell's
sacrifice for her humanitarian beliefs. She went to the aid of every

soldier in need of care, not judging by which side might have claimed him. Edith helped a couple hundred allied men escape the Germans in occupied Belgium. When a firing squad executed this brave woman, a rallying protest arose against this injustice, gaining world-wide attention to her name. I was but 15 years of age, but oh how my heart surrendered to the cause. I landed in the nearest recruiting station and signed on, as soon as the French nursing corps would accept me. By the end of that war, I was enamored with the good Dr. Alix Lefort, and my life took off in all those unexpected directions. So there you have it.

L: You leave me breathless, Cicely. Continue, please.

CL: I'm glad you've brought Diana and Noor into the arena. Noor and I certainly became close, due to the intense time we shared in training, even though it was only a few brief weeks. And I met Diana during those contemplative hours waiting for our departure to France. As you've reminded me, Lizzie, war has a way of bonding even the most unlikely personalities. But let's save that discussion for later, and would you please take out that bit about the three of us being childless! It doesn't seem necessary. I'd like to get back to the cruise. The cruise, I suppose, to end all cruises. (It certainly was our final cruise, most regrettably.)

Some time at sea was an extravagance we somehow felt was deserved. The world seemed to be heading toward some kind of division, and Alix and I decided to do something we had never allowed ourselves before—to escape, to forget, to live our lives as gloriously as we could, if just for a while. There was dissention between us, but I don't want to think about that now. Yes, the cruise was likely an effort to grow closer again, to try and narrow the distance. That's what couples do, right? Evade as an attempt to avoid. I felt a mix of rejuvenation and melancholy on the ship. Of course, it was such an enormous reminder of that cruise to the Orient that Mother and Granny and I had embarked on, and which ended so tragically.

I am becoming confused again. Did the cruise with Alix rejuvenate our marriage? Or was it too obvious an attempt at something else? I just don't know, now. Meeting the Pougets was like a breath of fresh air, and a much needed diversion from our intense focus upon each other. We connected with them instantly. I like that sandy seashell detail you added. It might even have been so. I don't recall when we first met their daughter, Janine, but she was a lovely young lady, and we bonded with her as well. That's as far as I have energy for again. My mind is muddy. Return to your travel agenda, *s'il vous plaît*, and the trip you were planning.

    L: So I shall.

February 11, 2007. Though I now know of the existence of Mme Lefort, I have no way of contacting her. For some reason, the excellent René has decided that, just my knowing that Mrs. Lefort exists and having the documents he sent from her, this is enough. He does not think I need to contact her; therefore, he withholds her address, saying, "You may put 'the end' to your research." Yet I know that in many ways, my work to find Cicely is now just beginning.

So, again, I search through names in Paris for a match, and come across one name out of all of Paris that is the same as Dr. Lefort's second wife! I already have plane tickets to travel to France the following month, as I feel the time has come to somehow get closer to Cicely, though I am not quite certain how. Worried about doing the wrong thing, but more afraid of doing nothing at all, I write a letter:

> *I do not know if you are Mrs. Alix Lefort. If Mme Dumont contacted you about my research of Cicely and you are who I seek, please write immediately, as I leave for Paris a month from today, about the time your letter would arrive....*

I wait, not even knowing if Mme Lefort lives in Paris or on the Brittany coast. Meanwhile, I prepare to travel. Then comes this surprising reply:

*February 25, 2007*
*Dear Elizabeth,*
    *I am Mrs. Alix Lefort, Doctor's second wife. Of course it will be nice to meet you and to talk about Cicely*

*Gordon. But I am leaving Paris.... I might be missing*
*you if you come to Paris on March 12. Actually, my*
*documents concerning Cicely are with Sigrún Lilja in*
*Iceland, who is also very interested by Cicely's life. I have*
*written for her to send them back to me. I am waiting for*
*them.*
*Yours sincerely,*
*J. Lefort*

CL: Well, you certainly display the Lefort resourcefulness. Go on,
Lizzie. Talk to me about the next part, when the Germans invaded Paris.
Everything we'd come to trust and know was beginning to fall around us.
Please, paint me a picture. Title it "Invasion."

# INVASION

St. Cast Villa.
*Lefort family collection*

**LEISURE DAYS OF SAILING,** Cicely's inherited passion for horseback riding, and Alix's routine medical practice, are coming to an end. In 1939, Doctor Lefort is called up to join the army as a medical captain. His medical office in a distinguished suite on Paris's Avenue Bosquet has become the residence of Cicely and Alix as well. Here the wide boulevard extends all the way to the *Pont de l'Alma* spanning the Seine. A stroll of only a few blocks takes them to the green expanse of the *Parc du Champ de Mars* leading to the *Tour Eiffel*, that wondrous iron armature representing revolution and freedom. But along these avenues, side streets and parkways, the usual sense of peace has been swept away. No longer can the Leforts wander casually arm in arm past decorated shop windows and strolling neighbors. All around are signs of distress. Boarded up shop fronts. Empty streets. Despair written upon the few passing faces. The alarming result of what could be called a lack of imagination consumes not only Paris but all of the European countryside as well: the failure to imagine what terror humans are capable of inducing. An inability to comprehend rumors too wicked to believe.

The anti-Semitism movement that has invaded Europe for decades becomes more flagrant. Joseph Goebbels, as Reich Minister of Propaganda, promotes the Jew as enemy in German school curricula that reaches from children's primers through to more advanced instruction, imposing Nazi flags and addressing "the Jewish Question." For after-school play, there is even a board game named "Jews Out!" to occupy developing minds.

Social Darwinism of the early 1900's has by now influenced the rise of German National Socialism, defined through the eugenics mentality of the Nazis. Even the French government turns away those who were once its own, forbidding French Jews to volunteer as soldiers against the tide of Germany pushing ever closer to invading their French borders. Already, Doctor Lefort must have patients and neighbors who are victims of racism and propaganda. The sweep to eliminate mass segments of humanity is reaching ungodly proportions.

June, 1940. Throughout Europe the second year of war is in full swing. France is in upheaval and, on the 14th of June, Paris falls into the hands of the Germans. On the 18th, through the BBC in London,

Charles de Gaulle puts out his call to resist Marshal Pétain's unacceptable surrender under the guise of an armistice. During the mass exodus from Paris, de Gaulle's nineteen-year-old niece, Geneviève, hears her uncle's plea over a loudspeaker. She stays in France and immediately takes up the cause of Résistance. Her path, too, will join Cicely's three years later on their journey toward Ravensbrück, the final destination for many women and political prisoners.

While Geneviève remains in France, the three women of British citizenship prepare to leave. Cicely is advised that as a British national in a German occupied country, she should immediately return to England. Perhaps realizing that remaining in France could compromise her husband's safety as well as distract him from his responsibility as a doctor, she acquiesces. Diana, also at risk as a British subject, engineers her departure from southern France to Britain through Spain and Portugal, while Noor escapes through Bordeaux to England. Soon these women, knowing nothing yet of each other's existence, will be entwined in a world of training and espionage and together will reenter the country they now reluctantly leave.

L: Cicely?

CL: I'm awake, dear, just have my eyes closed to help put me back in that time. My heart is speeding up already, though, anticipating what is to come. But don't worry. Really, I can't die again from this!

That mention of Geneviève. I did not realize at the time that this young woman who was on the transport with me on that god-awful journey to Ravensbrück was General de Gaulle's niece. What a brave soul she was, indeed. As prisoners, we were kept isolated from most news, and any whispers of this General that swept through the blocks did not have much context for us. Even now, what a story!

I see how valuable your take on these events is, with the benefit of history on your side. True, I actually lived it, but I did not have what I believe you now call "the big picture." Hmmm, we're making quite the team, I should say.

L: Indeed, my dear, indeed. I want to come back to correspondence between myself and James Close, or "Jimmy," as he begins to lead us into the war years. Keep in mind that not everything in the letters makes complete sense, and sometimes they in fact mislead us, but in light of this theme of spying and decoding, this scramble seems fitting. In the end, everything should fall into place, if we do our work right. Yes?

CL: That remains to be seen.

L: Don't decide to get tough on me now, Cicely.

Here are parts of a two-page letter I received from Jimmy on March 11, 2002. You might appreciate the blue ink from the fountain pen with which he often wrote.

*Dear Elizabeth,*

> *I have come across a book which recounts the careers of women who worked for the "Special Operations Executives," and who were flown to France to assist with sabotage against the Germans. A whole chapter is written about CL. I will send you a copy if I can find one.*

L: It is interesting to me that Jimmy refers to you, Cicely, as CL, for when I finally received a satchel of letters written between you and Alix during the war, your signature in every letter to your husband is CL, never Cicely. Comments? No? Maybe later. Here's more of Jimmy's letter:

> *It appears that she left her husband and France in 1940, to live in England as it was thought that if she stayed, she would be arrested. It is my intention to get copies of this book, of which I will send you one. She and her husband had a flat in Paris, and a villa on the Brittany Coast. The location is in this book. She sailed yachts.*

*With best wishes,*
*Jimmy*

L: And now I want to come back to my notes again (I hope I don't sound bossy!). There's something else I'd like to discuss:

Messages fly between me and Sigrún Lilja, the woman in Iceland who had Madame Lefort's documents. Sigrún has had a history-based interest with Cicely for a number of years. She made a trip to Paris to meet Mrs. Lefort, who then loaned her the documents, including letters written between Cicely and Alix during the early part of the war. As Sigrún and I get to know each other, we decide that, rather than impose again on Mrs. Lefort for copies, Sigrún will send a duplicate set of letters to me. It is through Sigrún Lilja's visit with Mrs. Lefort and my subsequent correspondence with Sigrún that I learn about Cicely and Alix meeting during World War I, that Cicely was a war nurse, and that Alix was a soldier and patient in the hospital.

When the bundle arrives from Iceland and I begin to read the letters, the world of Cicely and Alix opens to me. Besides significant war information, I get a feel for the concern and affection in their relationship. I am also aware that for all these years since the war, Doctor and Mrs. Lefort honored the life and memory of Cicely by keeping these letters and documents. This reinforces the need to continue the recovery of Cicely's life. In some sense, I wonder if my taking on the responsibility of revealing Cicely's history might be a relief to Mrs. Lefort, as she is no longer accountable for preserving the story of Cicely.

L: Cicely, can we talk? About Sigrún Lilja?

CL: I told you, dear. She provided a cerebral connection for many years. To say more than that, I prefer not. Not now. It will only confuse me. And it will definitely confuse you.

L: I will respect your wish, Cicely, after I just ask this: Can you tell me "why defer to her?" She's not family, so why is she so interested in your life, almost as much as I am? As you mentioned earlier, I am your bloodline. What does Sigrún have to offer?

CL: Let's just say that she knows things.

L: Now, don't you sound like a spy! Or, do you mean more like Corrie's brother, Willem, who "saw things"?

CL: Yes, that's closer to how it works. I believe Sigrún Lilja's interest began when she started to have dreams that reflected my time as a nurse during World War I. This manner of revelations is really not that simple, you must understand. This "tapping" can work both ways. That's enough for now. I want to stay in the present, the relative present. I mean World War II, and all that.

L: Just one more question (sigh): Sigrún has asked me more than once if it was ever possible that you had a child.

CL: I thought that had been established. Now, get back to the war.

L: Yes, Madame:

It's 1940. England. Cicely settles in and reconnects with relatives who live near London, expecting to wait out the war until she can return to France and her husband. By fall, the city will enter the era of the Blitz, besieged by night with the squeal of bombs, followed by that dreaded silence while waiting for the targets to be hit. Cicely stays with her cousin, Kitty Graham, whose mother is Susan Humble. Before the war, Kitty, too, shared a sense of adventure and established residency in Italy.

When the Italian port of Genoa is attacked by French destroyers, Kitty manages to get on a coal ship and escape, even as Cicely evades German U-boats (short for *Unterseeboot*, or "undersea boat") in the English Channel on her escape from France to Jersey on that night that she and Alix parted. Kitty's journey takes her through Gibraltar and Lisbon as she manages her way back to England. Here she rents a house called Square Acres on the Farnham Common, and this is where the lives of Cicely and Kitty intersect once more.

On September 22, 1940, settled at Square Acres—now relatively safe, with one of the few links to the family of her childhood—Cicely writes what may be her first letter to Alix since her flight from France.

CL: Oh how lost I would have been, were it not for my precious cousin Kitty. I do mean precious too, and you may not take that word away. She does indeed enter my life often. Dear, sweet, life-saving (literally) Kitty.

L: Yes, your cousin, Kitty. You didn't even realize how much you meant to her during your lifetime. She was very loyal to you, Cicely, and you'll be quite pleased with how she comes to honor Alix, in spite of the endings yet to come. We must both be better than we think possible, if you and I are to see this story come together. Well, it certainly is what it is. I guess it's just a matter of how we each want to accept the outcome; perhaps you more than I, to be sure.

CL: My letter to Alix, then?

*Sept. 22, 1940*

*My dear Alix, I have just received your two letters from July 24 and 26. I got two telegrams from you. I wrote to Anna in July but I haven't got any answer. I went to Jersey Island, from where I thought I could leave to come back. But Jersey was evacuated and I had to come here. Fortunately I had given Kitty's address to Anna. I thought only that I would write to Kitty if I had stayed in Jersey. Kitty is here. She came from Cannes to Gibraltar without difficulty. The nature of Kitty's cheque was worthless. Everybody asks news from you. What happened to the Privie family? I hope that Anna managed to get my bicycle, the one with green mud flaps that I left in the garage in Dinard. What happened to L'Ariane? I am going to send another letter to Paris. I wrote to Madame Reutz thinking that she could give me news from you. Mrs. Fox and René are here. Here the question of food becomes terrible. I see that your letters took almost two months to arrive. I got two of them at the same time.*

*I hope you are going to be able to take your mother to Paris. Mr. Barret's papers and the books from the attic are here. I hope to have other news soon from Anna. I didn't know that Limoges had been bombed.*

*All my affection,*
*C.L.*

CL: That's the actual letter. How did you manage that? My goodness. I was rather verbose, wouldn't you say? I suppose I still had time on my hands, before all the rest set in.

L: You see, I first read about *L'Ariane* from this letter. At the time, I didn't know what, or who, *L'Ariane* was. You'll be amazed at the documents I've uncovered—from the discoveries our dedicated René made and all the people he found to help, to your entire French dossier that I copied in Paris in the spring of 2007, and the full set of SOE documents a scholar from Trinity sent to me. You may now see why this gets so complicated. Especially so, once I had assimilated the English file, and saw how it, in so many ways, countered what I thought was the story from the French papers. (For example, dear Cicely, I had it in my romantic state of mind that the only thing in the world that mattered was for you and Alix to be reunited.)

But just hold on, that is all part of the story, and yet to come to light. I'd like to continue with my version of what was happening that year of 1940.

That summer of 1940, the Channel Islands of Jersey and Guernsey are occupied by Hitler's forces. Imagine Cicely, looking across the English Channel from Jersey toward the land that has been her home as a World War I nurse, a roaring-20's bride, a wife. Scanning the waters, Cicely must ache to discern a glow through the fog from the lights of France, only 20 miles away.

Each phase now will remove her further from that life and forward into a world she could never have imagined. Her return to war-inflicted England is not without peril, either. Amidst the chaos of bombings surrounding London, the beginning of the evacuation of two million children by rail and lorry into the safety of English countryside and foster homes, and the assault on her husband's country, Cicely's letters show a need to keep her thoughts focused on routine daily discourse. The constant difficulty to send and receive information continues. She sends duplicate letters to Alix through connections as far away as Portugal and eventually Canada and America, many of the letters undated and filled with seemingly uneventful sentiments.

> My Dear Alix,
>
> Don't forget to eat well. The roast beef from Albion made me gain 12 kg back. I hope your mother and brother might be able to join you at Avenue Bosquet. If you could, give me an address in unoccupied France. I have sent two letters day before yesterday. One at the address in Limoges and one to Paris.
>
> All my affection,
> C.L.

Autumn in England. Fair weather works in favor of Reich Marshal Goering's *Luftwaffe*, and night bombings threaten to overwhelm London, hitting targets as revered as Buckingham Palace. In the countryside, Cicely and Kitty witness the glow of fires through the Lindens and above the hedgerows. Within days of Cicely's posted letters, the Battle of Britain commences. But thanks to the vigorous Air Defence of Great Britain (ADGB) by the Royal Air Force (RAF), and with the new secret British weapon of radar, by late September the daytime attacks cease. Even though the threat of invasion recedes as Hitler's focus turns toward the Soviet Union, the Blitz continues to increase its targets, and civilian casualties and injuries mount monthly, upward toward 10,000. It is not until November 3, after 57 consecutive nights of air raids, that the residents of London experience one full quiet night, though the ten nights to follow again rain terror.

Meanwhile, in occupied France, all Jews are ordered to register with authorities. Every day, Alix might be forced to notice the disappearance of patients. Every day, citizens of France are warned by Maréchel Phillipe Pétain—soon to be recognized as the Chief of State of Vichy, the pro-Axis French government and a leader who should instill confidence—to put no value on friendships. Yet, under his control, all are suspect. Paranoia and suspicion thrive.

Throughout the end of 1940, physical and emotional destruction take their toll on the residents of both England and France. During this period of Cicely's life in England, some hope persists with Roosevelt's verbal support from the United States and his fireside chats, promising full aid to Britain. Will Christmas bring an even deeper depth of loneliness to separated families, both civilian and military? Or with so many missing, will the usually festive holiday be left unacknowledged?

The beginning of 1941 proves no different than the end of 1940. The war in Europe is relentless. Doctor's immediate world continues to crumble around him. Even in the midst of a war zone, with death on every side, Alix is devastated when his mother unexpectedly dies.

L: Here, though, is the next letter I have that you wrote to Alix, on April 1, 1941. His mother had just died in March, but you have not received the news yet. You write:

*April 1, 1941*
*My Dear Alix.*

*I haven't heard from you since January 15. I got a letter from you and from Isabella at the same time. I am with Aline. Renée and her husband come to see us often. Despite the weather I haven't had a serious flu or cold all of the winter.*

*My cousin Franklin wrote to me that he tried to send news to you. Mrs. Wood has a house in the countryside not far from here. She wanted me to live with her but I have better things to do. Aline can't hear any news from her family. I am wondering if your mother and Anna are still in St. Cast. I often hear news from Bobby and Lucy Brooks. How's Robert? It sounds like he found Louise again. It's sad for L'Ariane. I would like so much to have news from everybody. At last it will come.*

*All my affection,*
*CL*

CL: As you say, when I wrote that letter, I did not know that Alix's mother had already died. It breaks my heart to think of how alone Alix must have felt. Neither he nor I could realize that our messages continued to cross, so that by the time he received any news from me, and I from him, all had changed again. Even though we must have had some understanding of the ways of war correspondence, I suppose each in our own way also felt dismissed. I'll try to keep an open mind and see how this continues to play out.

L: Yes, let's continue. You are being most magnanimous, Cicely, and reflective in what I'm coming to learn is so much a part of who you are, and why you touched so many lives. Do I begin to catch a glimmer of boredom coming from you: "I have better things to do" than to settle into relative comfort in the countryside with Mrs. Wood? Here, though, is the letter to you from Alix, when his mother died, along with a breakdown of how messages were delayed and overlapped. He wrote this letter to you, two weeks after his mother died. You'll see that Anna also sent a telegram informing you of Alix's mother's death. Do you recall receiving it? I fear the contents might still be news to you. We'll see. This could be rough.

*March 21, 1941*

> *Very dear Cicely, I haven't heard from you for a month. The last news came to me through the Red Cross. However, I would need so much to have you close to me in the horrendous moments that I am going through. My poor mother died in St. Cast on Mar. 6 at 10:30 pm. I couldn't be close to her in her last moments. She who loved me so much, who adored me. She died all alone. Oh Cicely, how I cried and I am horribly unhappy. She was in good health until Mar. 6 at noon. The day before she wrote me a long letter telling me that she felt very well and that she was happy I was coming to visit. She rejoiced that I would come. Indeed, I intended to spend ten days with her at the end of the month of March, and at noon she became very ill. She felt sick and vomited, and suffered vomiting until 5 pm., and she was made very tired. At this time her heart must have failed and she passed away at 10:30 pm. During the afternoon she called, "Alix Alix Alix," and Anna, who was with her, told her that I would come. Unfortunately*

*telegrams are forbidden and Madame Lejune had to go as far as St. Brevin. She managed to flag down a messenger. I only received my telegram on Thursday at 1:30 p.m.*

*She was very beautiful on her bed. Her features were calm and rested. She didn't have any wrinkles any more and seemed to fly close to God. How I suffered alone my dear Cicely. I suffered so much that I fainted on the stone path of the garden and I cut my forehead and broke a front tooth.*

*Be very careful, because I don't want anything to happen to you.*

*But my God how difficult it is. Only telegrams reassure me by giving me recent news from you.*

*I kiss you with all my heart.*

*Alix*

L: Cicely? Are you all right? I'm so sorry. Perhaps this is too much. Shall we take a break?

CL: No, by all means, we're in this, it would be too hard to stop and have to come back. But goodness, I see how darling Alix was, and indeed, my general messages to him must have seemed dismissive. Perhaps I had withdrawn more than I realized. Consequence of war? Or just of a relationship in trouble? Most likely, both. No wonder....

I'd like to see now how jumbled our messages became. Maybe that will help.

L: I will point out, although this might add to your pain, how Alix underlined those words for you, to be so very careful? He really did adore you. I say that to help you feel better, though I understand how it might not work that way. I also believe that his overwhelming concern for you is why he felt you had so betrayed him once he understood your role with SOE, and by then, of course, it was too late.

So, this is how it goes: The same day that Alix wrote his letter to you — I suppose it was written from Paris — Anna transmitted a telegram to you from St. Cast. She sent this same message to Mrs. Brooks (related to the Closes?) in Washington, D.C.

> *I am still at St. Cast. Madame Lefort died on the 6th*
> *of March. Monsieur was unable to get there in time, he*
> *stayed ten days and is very unhappy.*
> Anna, March 21, 1941

L: Yes, Cicely, this message from Anna does sound curt, but I don't think you should read anything into it. Remember, telegrams sent through the Red Cross had a limit of 25 words and were to provide only the barest news of a strictly personal character. The telegram, written in March, was postmarked as having not arrived in England until June 9 and not delivered to you for another three weeks. So by the time you got any of this news, it was already four months old.

But coincidently, on April 1st, the same day you wrote the letter above, Alix also sat down and wrote another letter to you, regarding his mother's death. His letters give the feeling of a need to just hold on, to keep writing in order to feel connected.

*April 1, 1941*
*My Dear Cicely,*
> *How difficult it is to give you news from me. I have*
> *just written a letter to Mrs. Brooks. I received another one*
> *which I will try to get to you directly because I believe*
> *that through the postal box the letters don't seem to*
> *arrive. I wrote you at least 6 or 8 letters and I think that*
> *you must have written a lot as well. The best is to write to*
> *Madame Henri Le Clerc, and to Mrs. Beringer at the*
> *hotel Termal de Vichy. You should send me through these*
> *two persons a telegram each month so I will have recent*
> *news and I could be less worried.*
> *I got a letter from you through Madame Marche who*
> *must have sent it back to Madame LeClerc because Madame*
> *Marche didn't have any way to send it. I received the*
> *telegram for Madamaselle Meringer, then news for Mrs.*
> *Brooks and Franklin Humble. And then a letter from the*
> *Red Cross of Geneva dated Jan. 24, 1941 to which I*

*replied immediately... The last news was transmitted to
me by a letter you wrote to Janine Pouget but Janine is
not in Vichy anymore, she's now in Paris.*

*As you must have learned from my former letters, I
was very sad to lose my dear Maman. She died on Mar 6
1941. I couldn't even arrive on time to be there for her last
breath. It had been six months since I had seen her and
she rejoiced that I was coming to see her. What a terrible
sadness. I am desperate in my sad isolation. She loved me
so much, with a long devotion for her sons. And I am
alone to mourn. She stayed there waiting until I can bring
her back to be close to my father. And now I am alone.*

*Time goes by slowly and sadly. We have to be brave
and we will have better times later.*

*Good bye Cicely. I kiss you very tenderly.*

*All my affection,*
*Alix*

L: You see, Cicely, this is the letter where Alix mentions Janine
Pouget. This is how I realized that Janine is now Mrs. Lefort. Those
times of war were weary indeed, and deep loneliness might have been
unavoidable. And look, only two days later, Alix wrote yet a third letter
to you, desperate to send news and to hear anything from you.

*April 3, 1941*
*My Dear Cicely.*

*Do you get my letters? I doubt it. However, I write to
you as often as I can. At least every two weeks. But I
think that they don't get to you through the postal box.
Anyway, through this p o box I only got some letters. One
from Anna, one from Madame Diasach, and from Mrs.
Brooks who was kind enough to give me news from you
through Madame LeClerc. I will try again.*

*I also managed to get a letter from Franklin Humble
who offered me to pass on my letters.*

*I think that the best solution for me in order not to
worry, to be calm, would be that you send me a telegram*

*every month. Sometimes with the help of Mademoiselle Beringer to the Hotel Terminal or with the help of Madame Henry LeClerc. I will have more recent news and get less worried. I also heard news from you with the help of Mademoiselle Duzoire from New York, one of my former nurses who lives in America.*

*As you have probably heard, my very dear Maman died on Mar 6, 1941 in St. Cast and I couldn't be there to kiss her. I hadn't seen her for 6 months. I am extremely unhappy and desperate. She loved me so much. My poor Cicely, it's terrible.*

*Finally we need hope and courage, in order to go through these terrible hardships. I beg you, take all dispositions to be the most secure, safe as possible. I always go out each morning but time goes by slowly.*

*Good bye my dear Cicely. I kiss you very tenderly.*
*Alix*


L: These are love letters to you, Cicely.

CL: I believe you are correct, Lizzie. You know, I don't even remember now if I received all those letters. Look how many times he wrote the same news. Surely some must have survived the circuit. Sad to say, I don't recall which ones. And I'm quite certain I did not recognize, or appreciate, Alix's propensity for sentiment.

I'm so pleased to have an opportunity to remember Franklin. Please share the letter he wrote. It's been such a long time since I have thought about him.

# OVER THE POND

S.S "LEVIATHAN." 59.956 TONS.      UNITED STATES LINES
(THE WORLD'S LARGEST LINER)

*Leviathan,* the ship Cicely boarded from Europe
to America.
*Collection of Paul McCue*

L: **WELL, DEAR,** the reason that we are now able to read these letters is because your Alix, and then his lovely (new) family, kept watch over your papers and photographs for all these many years. That, too, is like a love letter, and the highest honor of respect for the life you and Alix did have.

Now, as to Franklin Humble. Cicely, I must admit, if it's not already obvious, that with all the lines and threads of Humbles and Closes and Gordons (and now and then a Brooks joining in), crossing over and doubling back, I do have trouble keeping track. But this Franklin, he is one of the two people I mentioned way back, as being a living person that you and I both knew in our own lifetimes (my sweet Grammie being the other one). I do remember meeting Franklin when my family drove to Victoria, BC, on a summer trip. It must have been around 1962, for I was about eight years old. I have this image of Franklin in the garden, and the moment I realized that his hesitant gait was related to the fact that, beneath this distinguished gentleman's pressed trousers, was a genuine wooden leg. Of course I had no clue this was a consequence of war.

Yes, I have a copy of a letter he wrote to you. It's quite full of news. I suppose that taking the time to write and post during the war did inspire commitment to fill in as much as possible. Here it is:

*July 1, 1941.*

*Dear Cicely, We live from one bulletin to another, and perhaps that is one of the reasons letters are delayed. Thank you very much for remembering the children in your will. I hope it will be very many years before that document is put into force. I heard from Dolly yesterday and she said you had gone back to Wales for a time.*

*The Hess incident is now past history but there is a rumour over here that he supplied us with some information about Hitler's intention to attack Russia. I feel sure that the main reason he flew to England was for the sake of his own hide primarily. He may have given the information to better his chance of saving his skin, but I doubt if it will help him in the long run; he has too many things chalked up against him in the big black book of jobs.*

*Did you ever manage to get in touch with your husband? Miss Little, who was going to forward your letters, wrote to say she had not as yet received any from you, perhaps you found some other method of getting in touch. I can write again through M. Le Clerc if you would like me to. Let me know next time you write.*

*We seem to be making good use of our time with air raids over Germany and northern France, the effect of those new bombs must be terrific. Pity we cannot fly across the Russian front and give the Germans over there a taste. What a pity it is we cannot change around, and give the people of England a period of rest over here. I am sure you have all got a good long period of leave coming to you.*

*Our garden is looking very nice just now, and we are picking our early peaches, from the looks of things we shall have a very big crop of plums, I have had to tie up all the branches so they will not break off.*

*The leading question here at present is conscription, the government got into power by promising not to bring in conscription but I think it would be welcomed now in the west; unfortunately the east does not want it and they count the most votes, and that goes a long way with politicians with an eye to the future. What they do not or will not see is that there may not be any future unless we put forward our greatest effort now.*

*I cannot get into anything to do with the war out here, age and disability are the reason. I am sure that if I were in England I could manage to get into something. It's all very disappointing to see the need so great and not be able to fit in somewhere.*

*The summer holidays have just begun, so I suppose occupation for the children is going to be the main topic for some time. I think Don is all for building a boat, I see they are going to have summer tennis so I may send them along there. We shall also do some fishing and get away for a week or two in August, that is if things do not take too bad a turn.*

*Hope you get the job you are after. Thank you again for your thought of the children. Take care of yourself and remember there will not always be a war on, and soon you will have the pleasure of kicking the Huns off your doorstep in northern France, and this time they must be kicked so hard they will never come back. Personally I would simply exterminate the race, they have had their chance and have kept Europe in a turmoil for the last forty years to say nothing of various other times since Caesar ruled the Romans.*

*Goodbye. Love from us all and the best of luck.*
*Your affectionate cousin,*
*Franklin*

L: That job Franklin mentions, Cicely, must have been your entry into the Women's Auxiliary Air Force, which of course led you to SOE, and on into the war. I find Franklin's use of the word "exterminate" curious, as that is entirely what was behind the Nazi intentions. There is also a sad note about Franklin's son, Don, building a boat that summer. A few years later this young man drowned in a boating accident, perhaps in the very boat he was building. The best of luck was not to be, was it?

CL: No, luck was irrelevant, as history reveals. (I'm deeply saddened to hear about Don. He seemed such a gentle boy.) But thank you for this memory of dear Franklin. Mother's brothers and sisters were a saving grace throughout my entire life. In spite of scandal, they each remained true. It is unfortunate indeed that when you met Franklin, you of course had no idea who I was, that I even had existed, nor would you have been old enough to understand, but still. Still! You and Franklin met. Knowing this is a comfort to me.

L: I'd like to come back to the present, to a letter I received from Mrs. Lefort. We established a casual first name basis early on, so from here on out, she is Janine. (It also seems strange if I refer to Janine as Mrs. Lefort, as throughout all my research about you, Cicely, you are the Mrs. Lefort. I did notice that Janine refers to you as Cicely Gordon, and never Cicely Lefort. Oh, the personal safety nets we create.)

Because Janine of course writes in French, I can only pick through bits and pieces of the letter myself, until I get set up with another translator. (I've been able to find a number of eager French speaking folks around where I live. This, too, is so fitting for this adventure we're on!)

Janine responds to questions I have asked of her. This letter happened to arrive at my house on your birthday, April 30.

> *April 23, 2007*
>
> *Chère Elizabeth, I knew Cicely only a little before the war. Doctor was alone since 1940. Doctor Lefort and she were friends of my parents. She was a very great lady. He was a regular visitor at my house during the war because we had a bit of food. My parents liked him a lot because he was charming and very simple. In 1940/41 letters were exchanged from Cicely in London. My parents met the Leforts during a cruise in the Mediterranean in 1936. I did not see Doctor and Cicely much at that time.*
>
> *Yes, my family is Pouget. How did you know that?*
>
> *Cicely had a lot of class. She was aristocratic and had friends from high society. She practiced horseback riding and sailing. Cicely was very smart and cultivated.*
>
> *Sent with my warmest greetings,*
> *Janine*

CL: How *did* you know her family was Pouget?

L: You've gotten rusty, dear Cicely. Don't you remember? It was when I came across Alix's letter to you, and he mentioned the Pougets. I noticed that the Pouget's daughter was named Janine, and I knew by then that Alix's second wife's name was Janine. I put two and two, you know, together, and then I asked Janine.

Janine's letter was another turning point for me to piece together that span of time that you and Alix had during your years together before the war, the second war. Some things were beginning to fall into place. I could retrace, and imagine that cruise and the significance of the friendship that formed between you, Alix, and the Pouget family, especially of course, Janine.

Soon after this letter, I received another note from Janine. This was June, 2007. She wrote:

> *After the war and death of Cicely, Doctor Lefort married me in 1946. There were 30 years between us, but he was a marvelous husband. We had together 3 daughters. My husband died in 1969. Cicely had no children.*

L: I know, Cicely, that you do know all this by now, but I still feel odd just tossing the reality out there. Alix became the father of three daughters! This might pain you on some level, but on another note, it is beautiful in so many ways.

CL: It is, beautiful, and yes, painful. I understood that Alix wanted very much to be a father, but being a devoted mother just wasn't part of my constitution. This became the biggest hole in our marriage. I think I see now just how immense a hole it made. I believe I am, or was, just not the nurturing type, not enough anyway.

Look at those brief messages I sent to Alix, while he was tossing his heart out to me across the waters of war. I must admit, when I wrote to Alix, I didn't realize how distant my messages sounded. Yes, yes it is sad. But, as I believe some say, "it is what it is," and in so many ways it is the undeniable truth.

L: I'm relieved to hear that from you, Cicely. When Janine shared her family photographs of their daughters (who, by the way, are all about my same age), and as I connect with her family in ways that would have remained unknown to me were it not for your story, I become a witness to the good that comes out of tragedy. I felt a sense of atonement. The sadness that I had been harboring about your death lessened. Not the tragedy of your death, nor the waste, the regret, the finality of lives affected by these war crimes. These did not lessen, but I felt able then to celebrate more fully your life, and honor your death.

I just had another thought, Cicely. I think you need to give yourself more credit here, too, as far as the brevity of your messages to Alix, and how they might have been misinterpreted as not caring. You were, dear Cicely, secretly training for the mission of returning to France, into the center of war, and no one—not Kitty, not Alix—*no one* could know about that. So perhaps your, shall I say "bland," messages were quite necessary, for self-protection, to protect Alix as well from being put in a compromising situation, and for the entire war effort.

Don't you see that, now?

CL: Thank you for that grace, Lizzie. Thank you.

L: Here is part of another letter from Alix to you, written that spring of 1941:

> *I knew that you had lived with Eve where she lives because of the situation in the mts. I will feel a bit more calm, less worried, if you stay with Eve and do not attempt to go to the U.S.A. It is safer than at your aunt's house. Anna has always stayed in St. Cast. It's not very prudent because if the house isn't occupied, nothing will remain of it.*
>
> *I am desperate in my sad isolation. And I am alone to mourn. Time goes by slowly and sadly. The beautiful times went away.*
>
> *Au revoir, Cicely. I kiss you very tenderly. Toute mon affection,*
> *Alix*

L: What does he mean about going to the U.S.A.? I suspect you were playing with possibilities of how to explain any extended absence to him, the lack of correspondence that you anticipated, once you entered France as an agent. Being clever? What turmoil you must have been feeling, to have to deceive your husband in order to carry on; a cost of war on your marriage, as well. Or did you indeed plan to travel to America, and when that fell through, your desire to increase activities took hold? I do have to wonder, because that's what I do, just what reason you might have had to even consider travel to America during that time of war? I must think there was a deciding factor.

CL: I ask you to stay with your initial suspicion, Lizzie, as to why Alix might have referenced travel to U.S.A. So please, provide an overview of that time when I did join the Women's Auxiliary Air Force. I did not of course have this historic perspective, as it was all so new and was just developing while the war progressed. We saw only what was right in front of us, day to day. Enlighten me, if you will, and forget about America.

L: It is June, 1941. By now, Cicely, you have considered a future with the Women's Auxiliary Air Force (WAAF). It could be that existing without focus or direction is not acceptable to a woman like you, accustomed to days in the countryside along the Brittany coast or the city avenues of Paris. Perhaps this resumption of life in England sparks nostalgia for your childhood, running in the rose gardens with your Chow companions, but the adult Cicely can't indulge in such play. The next time Alix receives news from you, you have joined the WAAF. Here is an historical overview, as you have requested. Forgive my "lecture" mode, but for facts, this works.

Formed in June 1939, the Women's Auxiliary Air Force had earned respect for its thousands of members, with involvement in over 50 trades from loading coal to loading bombs, packing lunches to packing parachutes, controlling barrage balloons to collecting coffins. Your work as a nurse during WWI will be appreciated. I also suspect, especially knowing you more personally by now, that for you and for other WAAF recruits, it might simply have been boredom, and the loss of attachment to family, that led to recruitment.

While your WAAF training was in its infancy, in Paris as well as across Europe Résistance movements took up another call for victory, defiantly painting V for victory across vacant walls and German posters. Alix might have rallied upon viewing continual insurgence in the face of invasion, hoping that each mark of subversion was one infinitesimal step closer to the end of the war, the return of his wife, and the life you both had hoped for.

CL: Well done.

L: Here is a letter to you from Alix, dated July 23, 1941. At least some of your messages are being received, but his words reflect a tone of discouragement, and notice that he does not close with endearments.

> *I am very glad because I received one of your letters. I didn't receive any letters from you after June 25. The last two letters were from May 30 and June 5. I haven't received any telegram for a long time. Don't leave me without news. I am so tired because I am alone to look after the entire hospital, but vacations on the coast are forbidden. I hope that you have good health and you don't suffer too much. Here it's rather terrible. Meat is almost impossible to find.*
>
> *We all hope for a better time.*

# II. DES DÉCISIONS RAPIDES

Tangmere Control Tower marks the airfield where SOE agents
departed for occupied France.
*Collection of Paul McCue*

# THREADS

Cicely Lefort in WAAF uniform.
*Lefort family collection*

**L: I LOST TRACK OF YOUR MOVEMENTS** for about a year here, Cicely. Without letters found between the previous one of July 1941, and a brief note dated October 1942, while conflict indeed raged on, it was hard to pick up the thread of your journey.

Forgive me for not entirely letting this one thing go, but I suppose that had you pursued a plan to visit America, this year would have provided the time to do that, before you became entrenched with the war effort. Even though Alix appeared to have made a reference to that prospect, for the life of me I don't see how that would be at all possible, given the consuming turmoil of the world.

Hope still held a stronghold for many throughout the year that stretched from Alix's August 1941 letter, and the next evidence of correspondence in a brief note from Cicely to Alix in October of 1942.

August of 1941 announced the meeting of President Roosevelt and Prime Minister Winston Churchill for five days aboard the Prince of Wales, a ship that would be sunk by the Japanese that December. On the Prince, they signed the significant Atlantic Charter, securing the United States and England as Allied Powers.

September of this year held other relevant events. The Channel Islands, including Jersey, were overwhelmed by collaborators. Had Cicely remained in Jersey where she first escaped from France a year earlier, she would most likely have been among the thousands of undeclared resistance followers who found their lives upended with restrictive rules, fines, and starvation. But England was not far from these upheavals. A mainstay of food for Cicely and Kitty would be potatoes as a result of the "Potato Pete" campaign. Citizens were encouraged to fill up with these unrationed edible tubers.

In France, Alix would witness more disturbing campaigns, such as the pervasive *Le Juif et la France* (The Jew and France). Banners and posters as monstrously tall as three stories of a building depicted Jews as clawing, evil, criminals. By October, Paris had few if any Jews remaining; most had either died or been exiled to the ever growing ghettos. This same month, the physically removed Charles de Gaulle made a valiant plea for French Résistance sympathies to cease their attacks on Nazis, hoping for an end to relentless German reprisals.

By December, back in England, all unmarried British women from 20-30 were called to public service. Cicely would not have qualified for this rule, by both limitations, but her time to serve was still to come. In Germany this same month, Hitler began the darkly named campaign, *Night and Fog*. Mysterious disappearances began to occur to anyone who threatened the ideals of Nazi Germany.

Even more destructive and consuming attacks were secretly underway. The seventh of December's day of business began under its own fog of security over the U.S. Pacific fleet based in Pearl Harbor. Just as breakfast would have ended in Hawaii, and lunch was well over in Washington D.C., all hell broke loose. Light was obliterated from the sky, and the waters of the harbor turned black with smoke, bombs, oil and blood. Surely this important news reached both Cicely in London and Alix in Paris within hours, if not moments, of each other.

On December 11th, the U.S declared war on Nazi Germany and Italy. Eight days later, Hitler became commander-in-chief of Germany. Across Europe, the war front headed into a bitter, frozen winter.

The first half of the year 1942 raged on in the Battle of the Atlantic, on the Eastern Front, North Africa, and the Mediterranean, as well as across the expanse of Europe. British Air Operations' RAF division gained public confidence and intensified its bombing offensive, proving its worth against Germany. Throughout spring and into summer, it was evident that most of the world would be impacted by this war.

CL: Such drama all around the world. There is, sadly, much truth to human foible. Now, the note, if you please?

L: Yes, dear. Here is the message that you penned to Alix, toward the end of fall in 1942. You manage to remain neutral and withhold anything significant about the events of the past year that were crucial to the outcome of the war.

*My dear Alix,*

   *I got a letter from you in August and then nothing. I hope that you are doing well. I tend to be worried for the news is scarce. I am doing very well. I saw Kitty the other*

*day. She wrote to you as well. Renée Fox is expecting a*
*baby. I think that this winter will be long.*
*Toute mon affection,*
*C.L.*

CL: As I wrote: news was scarce!

L: That is was, Cicely. By this time the United States was fully engaged in battle and war efforts had escalated. No longer can a quick end to war be even remotely expected. Within a few months of your neutral October letter, your fluent French is brought to the attention of Special Operations Executives (SOE). Your recruitment might also have provided a further stage of hope for the possibility to return to France, along with the opportunity to be reunited with Alix (but this might just be my own romantic impulse imposed again). Yes, this winter would be long, but longer ones will follow.

CL: This is a fascinating process, Lizzie, seeing how my life moved along so precariously, from one happenstance to the next. Let's both step back for a while and let history run its course. Bring in a third-person perspective for this section, so you and I may sit side by side and take it all in objectively. I believe another pot of elusive tea is in order. I admit that just the thought of holding a cup of steaming Earl Grey is soothing to me. (I do rather enjoy this intangible aspect of our camaraderie. We seem like children, setting up our playtime tea setting.)

L: Or perhaps the warmth of some sherry, as long as we're fancying. Disregard the playtime table!

CL: *Mais oui.* Biscuits? *Merci.*

L: *Voilá!* What? You're smiling.

CL: Oh, I have always been tickled with the way non-French speakers love to insert a *Voilá* every now and then, as if it counts for speaking the language.

L: Fair enough. *Touché!*

CL: *Précisément.* Now please, continue.

While the majority of the Women's Auxiliary Air Force members remained in England, there were those few, such as Cicely, Noor, and Diana, whose enlistment through WAAF represented merely a stepping stone to another level of the war effort. Once these women's fluency in French was discovered—as well as their insiders' knowledge of French habits and landscape—their usefulness to the cause of Résistance took on new meaning through their appointment to Special Operations Executives.

F Section, one of the two French branches of SOE, was comprised of loyalists who despised the Germans but also did not overly favor de Gaulle's self-imposed agenda. All transactions with him would be carried out in French, even while he was in exile on British soil. In 1941, Colonel Maurice Buckmaster became the mastermind behind F Section. Buckmaster took his job for what it was, a matter of life and death for his agents. At times during training, Buckmaster took on the role of a Gestapo agent, interrogating recruits. Sometimes the hopeful agents stood naked for hours, withstanding cruel and persistent cross-questioning, while the stand-in "Gestapo" tried to break their resolve. If agents emotionally survived such rigor without collapse, their consolation was the confidence gained that could possibly save their lives, and others, if the enemy truly did get hold of them.

By early 1943, when Cicely, Noor, and Diana joined SOE, not a year had passed since women had been approved to be agents in Europe. Leaders had finally realized that the Gestapo would be less suspicious of women being out and about on the streets than of men. Of the 400 SOE agents who would be sent into France, 39 would be women. At that time a woman named Vera Atkins, F Section's Intelligence Officer, kept a special eye on the female agents of F Section.

Agents of SOE were sent to all Nazi occupied countries throughout Europe, and the agents sent to France worked especially closely with the French Résistance. Atkins aided the women in taking on a homely look, insisting that the women who went to France were devoid of beauty, looking as ordinary as possible; ordinary women performing extraordinary assignments.

Often, a woman's first contact was not with her knowledge of possible intentions. She might have been called in for an interview to 64 Baker Street, supposedly to be an interpreter or a bilingual secretary. Curiously for Cicely, this imposing building was only 13 doors away from the Alfred Ellis & Walery photo studio that her mother had taken her, with her Chow, 40 years earlier. The dark hallways and bustling activity surrounding the initial introduction would be nothing at all like that summer day's cheerfully lit photo session had been when Cicely was but a child.

During the interview process, Cicely, as a potential recruit, would be diverted into speaking French instead of English, a test of her fluency. The interview would take a subtle turn and become an interrogation. Her knowledge of French would be thoroughly tested, her background stringently analyzed, her motives and loyalties explored. She would be questioned as to what she thought of Germany and why she left France to return to England. She would be allowed to leave, with no explanation of the reason for the strange interview. Then, just as unexpectedly, she would be called back for a second meeting.

There would be even more urgency this time, a feeling of secrecy and collaboration. And the realization that, finally, there might be a way out of England and back to France. A third return would allow a prospect such as Cicely to accept or decline the offer. The terms: to withstand torture, to keep silent, even to death, should that be required. To have made it this far was an indication of commitment to the cause, and Cicely accepted the challenge to become an agent.

Though it took years for professional spies to train, during war time the agents of SOE received only a few months of training, beginning with two to four weeks at the Preliminary Special Training School. For Cicely, Noor, and Diana, as part of F Section heading to France, this special training took place in a large Tudor house called Wanborough Manor. The gardens, private park, and party atmosphere worked as camouflage from curious neighbors for what transpired behind the stone walls.

Constant assessment took place regarding the agents' ability to hold liquor and not talk, to speak exclusively in French, to provide no reasons for suspicion lest they be asked to drop out of the program altogether. This protocol was crucial to protect themselves and the entire espionage enterprise. If captured, agents were expected to maintain silence for a minimum of 48 hours, even under torture. This withholding of information would allow their particular networks to disperse and avoid exposure and capture. It was reported that the Gestapo were not particularly intelligent. They would never know as much as they let on to know during ruthless interrogation. If they really knew that much, they would not have the need for more information. Silence must be maintained, to protect the lives of their comrades.

During Cicely's training, she met an agent named Erwin Deman. As the son of wealthy Hungarian Jews, he had lived at times in Vienna and Budapest. Like Cicely's husband, Alix, Deman's father had also fought in World War I. His father's years as a POW in northern England ironically bred in him a deep affection for England. When Deman dropped into France in July, 1943, one month after Cicely's return to French soil, he was able to hide his Jewish ethnicity and pose as an insurance agent living in Rennes. Having reasonable cause for travel, he obtained a security pass for the coastal region.

A conversation between Cicely and SOE naval officer Captain Peter Harratt proved serendipitous. Once Harratt learned of the secluded beach just below the Leforts' St. Cast villa, he passed this information on to Deman and a strategy was set in motion, aided by the privileged knowledge of a family heirloom. Imagine Anna's surprise when a stranger knocked upon the villa door, having in his possession Cicely's inherited Celtic ring that was given to him as a way to identify himself to Anna! During the next few months, Deman operated the successful Var escape route between this beach and a more western beach near Morlaix, allowing nearly 70 men and women to enter and exit the area without capture.

CL: Very fine, Lizzie. Thorough. Particular. Factual. All right, so we are both aware that the third person narrator above is you, having removed yourself for an objective interpretation. Again, I am curious, and impressed, by some of the details you include, such as Buckmaster's interrogation methods, and to be privy to the party atmosphere surrounding Wanborough Manor as a way to divert suspicion from our real cause.

L: *Merci,* Cicely. Here is another detail that proves the importance of relationships that were established during the time of war: Erwin Deman was so moved and impressed by his mentor, Peter Harratt, that after Harratt died, Erwin adopted the name Peter to honor his compatriot. Erwin Deman remained Peter Erwin Deman for the last 30 years of his life.

I'm thankful you are curious about such details. It gives me a chance to bring in yet another "collaborator," shall I say, who I had the honor to meet in France in 2007, and who also helped me find you. Let's go back to my notes I made after I returned from that spring research trip. However, as is my prerogative, I shall update and personalize this by addressing you in my writings. As it was, you seemed to be very much a part of this meeting at the time.

Mrs. Riols greeted us at the swinging gate of the stone wall beside her house at the edge of the Marly le-Roi forest, along with her aging chocolate Labrador Retriever, Jesse. My daughter Margot, at age 13, and Jesse became fast friends. Most of our time spent in this quaint French home, the two of them made their own conversation, sprawled upon the tapestried carpet after Mrs. Riols escorted us into the sitting room. Mrs. Riols and I selected upholstered armchairs side by side, while my friend and editor Pamela and my interpreter Cecily (what a coincidence!) prepared to chime in from a daffodil-yellow settee. But first, English tea and daisy-edged biscuits were called for.

Mrs. Riols was every bit the vision of an English lady—wool skirt and cashmere sweater, stockings, and a necklace of pearls. She said that she had not met you, Cicely, but she did work with Noor and she knew other contacts with whom you worked. We began discussing Noor as we worked our way toward you.

She described Noor as a special and beautiful woman. Also, being quite frank, Mrs. Riols said that Noor did what was necessary—she slept her way through the ranks. "What an awful bloody mess she was when she was finally executed."

She mentioned a film that was made about Noor as being such a princess, but that it was a "load of crap," meaning that Noor was diligent, not spoiled.

Mrs. Riols also believed that Noor should never have gone to France as an agent, "But the decision was Buck's." During training sessions in Scotland, the sergeant told Noor to just get a hold of the gun and shoot, to which Noor said, "I will never kill, I will never tell a lie."

"She was a poet," Mrs. Riols said of Noor. "She just wasn't capable of the deceit that was necessary."

She went on to talk about the training, details I was happy to hear first hand from a person who had really worked it. Yes, I was talking to history! And to realize that I was also talking to someone who knew people who knew you. It just made this all seem so much more real.

Now, back to your transition, Cicely. To immerse you in the region into which you would be dropped, each of you exchanged all your English clothing for French attire, down to every last detail. The set of a collar, buttons, even men's trouser turn-ups had to be according to French fashion. Mrs. Riols recalled that SOE employed a Viennese Jewish refugee who was a tailor to tend to such details, right down to stitching and thread.

There were only ten moonlit nights a month when agents could be dropped into France. At first I wondered, "Why moonlight?" thinking it should be dark to sneak in. Then I understood that the pilots used only the light of the moon to follow their course and slip into enemy territory as unobtrusively as possible. If there was fog up over the Channel, you couldn't fly. Sometimes agents waited for five nights, all hopped up and expecting to be dropped in as weather allowed, only to miss the window of opportunity and be forced to wait for another full moon.

And then Mrs. Riols talked about you.

She knew that your code name was Alice, and said that you would also have had a French name—she didn't know what it was— but an historian I am even now working with on your life story recently informed me that the French name you were given, along with a false ID, was Cecile Marguerite Legrand (a clever restructuring of each of your real names, I must say). She said that agents usually had three names on file between the English and the French; a code name, a field name, and a false ID name.

Your delivery by Lysander, a British army liaison airplane, would involve a reception committee on the ground, four torches or fires to light a flare path, and a light to flash a code letter confirming that the scene was secure. The plane came in alongside the torches or fires, often not even stopping its engine, unless an agent was due to leave and was late. She knew that your flight was with Diana and Noor.

I mentioned that Henri Déricourt was part of your reception committee, and Mrs. Riols sat taller in her chair and abruptly said, "Oh, she was one with Déricourt? Well then, she didn't stand a chance. He was a double agent."

CL: Oh my, I think I need to catch my breath. Even though I did indeed live this, the telling of it now is so thrilling! The suspense has even me invested again. That Déricourt was a piece of work. Even though, as far as I knew then, his double crossing did not directly relate to my capture, the very mention of his name certainly indicated doom.

L: Oh yes, I know! I feel nervous and almost dizzy, as if I too am reliving the story. Sometimes now I begin to believe that the ending of this whole story might change, even though I know full well that's not possible. (Although, I must say, stranger things have happened.)

When I met Mrs. Riols in 2007, many of the war documents and files had only just been released into the public domain. They had been locked from public review until 60 years after the war ended. I suppose that even talking to me before this would have been forbidden for Mrs. Riols. In fact, I think she mentioned something to that effect. This is why, Cicely, so much of the tangle of information about you, and between you and Alix, was not understood. This is why, now, I can help clear up misunderstandings. The ending will be the same, but at least there's some reason for the way things fell in line or, for the most part, fell apart.

Mrs. Riols explained how pleased she was, once the records were opened, to find out that, for all the years since the war ended, the agent Pearl Witherington, who married and became Madame Cornioley, lived on Victor Hugo in Paris, just across the street from where Mrs. Riols's husband, Jacques, was born. During the war,

Jacques was in Général de Lattre de Tassigny's First French Army, fighting his way across France and Austria, into Germany.

During our visit that lovely afternoon, Mrs. Riols kept looking for a photo she had taken with Pearl at a reunion of agents at SOE headquarters. They could all finally get together because these 60 years have passed. "Now where is Pearl? I'll find her," she kept saying. "Oh, I'm still looking for Pearl. She always wears a black hat and a black coat." Just before we left that afternoon, Mrs. Riols said, "I'm sorry, Pearl's gone home."

"You'll find her when we leave," I said.

"Oh, the instant you leave!"

Maurice Buckmaster was at the reunion. What a scene that all must have been. I tell you Cicely, what I would have done to know more than I did, to have been able to attend and meet these amazing people, with whom you had worked. Perhaps in another life, as well. (As I said, stranger things have happened!)

Mrs. Riols remembered, during the war, when Terry (Terence) Kilmartin dropped into France without permission. "Buck came in and asked, 'Where's Captain Kilmartin?'"

Silence.

"Well, he dropped into France last night."

"I'll have him court-martialed!"

Buckmaster and Kilmartin met again at this reunion, after so many years, and became friends. She also noted that Bob Maloubier ("Gorgeous, handsome great fun!") had been living only two villages away all that time. "He personally blew up six bridges to stop the Germans from getting to Normandy. He went into the water and put fuses underneath. He's now on his third wife."

Once records were released, agents were able to find their compatriots again, and Mrs. Riols could talk about how she trained (and tricked) agents in training. She remembered one handsome man in particular. (I hope this isn't boring you, Cicely?)

CL: Oh no, not at all! We all had ideas of being deep in that world of espionage and secrecy; the drama, and yes, the romantic notion of it all. *Je l'adorais.* To hear about my fellow agents' lives so very long after the war, how much that time in our lives truly did matter, is more than I could have hoped for. Continue. I insist.

# PREPARING TO LAND

Wanborough House where many SOE agents trained.
*Collection of Paul McCue*

L: SO, MRS. RIOLS (you might have noticed that I refrain from using her war time name, just in case?) had staked herself out in a fancy hotel and appeared to be a single woman looking for a night of fun. This man, "Oh, he was gorgeous, and obviously smitten with me," asked her if they could meet, and he became amorous. When the flirtation ended and he found out that he'd been set up (remember, he was an agent in training, and being tested), he was asked by the back-up agents, "Do you know this woman?"

Mrs. Riols bluntly told us that he spewed, "You bitch."

The commandant replied, "If you can't resist a pretty head here, you're in danger over there, even after six months training."

Mrs. Riols said she wrote a book about all that, but because the files weren't open yet, she had to make it a novel.

I have since heard, though, dear Cicely, that Mrs. Riols's account has now been published without the label of fiction. I must make a point to find it and read it. Another example of doors that have opened now that the 60-year ban has been lifted.

She also worked with Kim Philby, later depicted in Britain's film noir thriller, *The Third Man*. Philby was a double agent who defected to Russia. "He was gorgeous, charming, everybody loved him." Other agents whose cover had been "blown" had to get out of the field fast, and they became trainers. A former burglar trained SOE agents how to pick every kind of lock possible.

"I wanted to put the whole thing behind me. But you can't. The war stays with you."

After the war, she tried to start over, sold everything, went to Bucharest, but had only enough money for a train ticket to Paris. "Oh, I got engaged a couple times and that didn't work." She got German measles, was offered a job in a press agency, and stayed. She met Jacques at the BBC.

And if I ever get to London, Mrs. Riols said she would be delighted to take me to the Special Forces Club, founded after the war by former SOE agents and staff. Your portrait is on the wall leading up the stairway, Cicely.

"You can only go with a member. It's easier to get into Fort Knox than the Club. I couldn't find the bloody place. It's just behind Harrods," Mrs. Riols explained.

She asked a doorman at Harrods if he could tell her where the Special Forces Club was.

"Do you mean the Secret Club, Madame? Were you *one of them?* Oh, allow me to shake your hand, Madame."

"So I allowed him," she chuckled.

I asked about de Gaulle. Mrs. Riols mentioned that Churchill believed that the Cross of Lorraine was the hardest to bear because it was so political. (Forgive me, Cicely, but I am not up-to-snuff on the notions this symbol represented, though I do understand that if one were not a follower of de Gaulle, the Cross of Lorraine would be disarming.)

Mrs. Riols explained how de Gaulle worked against French Section missions because of his need to control. Every message he sent had to be decoded. British agents were not even allowed to speak English to him in London. De Gaulle insisted that everybody spoke French, even though he knew English.

"Yes, he could be very difficult," she declared.

Mrs. Riols appeared in two films made about the war: *Secret Agent* and *Spy Master*. She eagerly reported how pleased she was because she was quoted more times in the films than de Gaulle.

"I checked!" she said with a twinkle.

CL: Fascinating. I'm sorry that I didn't have the pleasure of working with this fine lady. But may we take a little breather, now?

L: Of course, Cicely. I might have gotten carried away. But before we do, I want to mention something else I have noticed. (Don't look so suspicious, my fine first cousin.) You are beginning to sound a lot like me, or should I say perhaps, like an American? You seem to be losing that proper British edge. Is that fair to say?

CL: Interesting note, dear first cousin, twice removed! You do pay attention to detail, though indeed family trees seem to befuddle you. But now that you mention it, I'd have to agree. I believe this vernacular transition harkens back to my spy days. We had to adapt to whatever guise was necessary, at any moment's notice. I'm not too surprised that I'm already picking up on your modern dialect. Should I apologize?

L: No need to apologize, though I do rather enjoy that aristocratic mystique about you. Of course, you haven't lived in England for a long time now.

CL: No need to remind me.

L: Right. You rest a few minutes while I go back over my notes and see where we left off, before the Mrs. Riols excursion, fascinating as it still is! I shall look:

Stacks, heaps, piles. Boxes, containers, packages. Books? Oh yes. And letters, journals, memos. My resources are endless, and still growing. Even after the last symbol is typed to complete this manuscript, I have no doubt that there will be more messages, more to discover, more revealed. But one document at a time. Here now, the letter I was looking for.

CL: I'm ready. *Merci.*

L: *D'accord.* I received another letter from Jimmy Close, back in 2002 at the beginning of all this. Even then his comments verify what was yet to be discovered. March 27, 2002. Jimmy writes from his estate in Surrey:

*Dear Elizabeth,*

*Well, here is the book (Mission Improbable)! You should read right through, as it gives information about preliminary training, and how they found out about the careers of those who died. As for Cicely, one feels that brave though she was, she was not cut out for the job. She seems not to have been well, as it emerged later that she had cancer, and I think too that she was too old for this sort of thing.*

*One thing I am mystified about, is that she evidently gave a false maiden name (Mackenzie), and this curious story of being brought up in Ireland. Perhaps she felt that if she gave her true name of Gordon, there might have*

*been eyebrows raised as a result of the scandal, which
must have been well known.*

CL: I think I know you well enough by now, dear Lizzie, to
know what you're going to ask. I'll tell you right now, I don't want
to talk about it!

L: Irish? Mackenzie? It might help explain your Celtic ring that
Deman had in his possession to give to Anna so the agents could set
up the Var escape line. The mysterious Irish connection even
inspired a scholar from Dublin to contact me, asking if I'd like to
come to Ireland and present a paper on you! But alas, I had to
confess that as far as I know, there is no Irish connection. (Quite
frankly, I was relieved. The idea of presenting in Ireland terrified
me!) But Scottish, of course, because of Granny (or Eric, whichever
the case may be)! Still, none of this explains the use of Mackenzie as
your maiden name. Perhaps Jimmy is right, and it was merely an
attempt to discourage repercussions from your flamboyant childhood.
Please note, I have not asked you a question about any of this (yet).

CL: But you're not going to let it go, are you?

L: No, dear Cicely. I have a feeling there's more to this story. By
now, you must have realized that I've dealt with mysteries a number
of times during my research, sometimes from multiple sources at
once. As it turns out, you yourself are good at creating an aura of
mystery. I'm sorry, my friend, but this is what I do, too!

CL: So be it. But for now, a reprieve, *s'il vous plaît*. Get back to
the history, and take the third-person objective angle again. That
does take the pressure off us both.

Cicely, Noor, and Diana received specific training. Each would
be prepared for one of the main functions that their eventual teams of
three were to perform. They would not be part of the same organization
or circuit. Noor would have the most vulnerable position as a wireless
transmitter, and Cicely and Diana were to be couriers, relaying messages

(usually orally) as a liaison between local supporters and the organizer of their circuits. By the time they were ready to go, every detail of England would have been erased.

Final preparation involved the creation of new identities. This included working with their contacts to invent a plausible family history, occupation, and place of birth—information that would be tested on them when they faced a final mock Gestapo interrogation. Each held the deep-seated hope that they would never be put to the real test, though many finally were. Those who slipped at this point were allowed a cooling off time of isolation in Scotland, and then quietly released from the organization.

A date and plan for departure was arranged, with the hope for clear skies beneath a full moon. These flights were made by the appropriately named Moon Squadrons. One final visit to the office at Baker Street delivered the agents before Maurice Buckmaster. He knew each agent by name and face. For the women, a gift such as a silver compact would be given to them, the men perhaps a silver cigarette case, gestures of good will as well as later an item to pawn for trade should that become necessary.

If anything unexpected occurred, such as bad weather over France or England, obstacles at the chosen drop zone, or suspicion of German-infiltrated reception committees, the plan was scrapped and anxious agents had to come down off the high of expected departure, return to a holding house, and wait perhaps for the next quarter-wax to quarter-wane moon phase before preparing again for their descent into enemy territory.

On June 16, 1943, the moment for action arrived. Assigned to the same departure operation—a double Lysander mission labeled Operation Teacher—Cicely, Noor, and Diana would report to Baker Street where Colonel Buckmaster delivered his farewell words and his usual gift worth trading for information or help. With their plain luggage lacking any hint of English character and packed with only French fabrics and toiletries, they traveled by car to a cottage near Tangmere in Sussex, by the sea. Most of the shorter journeys into France by Lysander departed from Tangmere. Here they would spend their last hours and final meal on English soil, no doubt feeling a mix of anxiety and excitement. With final instructions memorized for adventures unknown, this trio of women agents prepare for their departure, bidding farewell to their pasts as they vow to embrace their futures, each with a new identity. Did these invented lives bring a taste of freedom for the capable women who volunteered?

Diana Hope Rowden, to be known from that hour forward as agent Madeleine, would divert from a life path similar to Cicely's in many ways. Also born in London and raised in France, Diana's passion for sailing mirrored Cicely's. She was, however, more defiant and rambunctious than Cicely, having had to keep up with two brothers. When her family moved from France back to England, when Diana was twelve, she became so unhappy that her mother eventually took her back to France to live.

When the Germans occupied France, Diana remained, even after her mother's escape by coal boat back to England. A year later, Diana saw the necessity for her withdrawal as well, and in the summer of 1941 arranged her own escape through Spain and Portugal. Her subsequent commission in the WAAF soon segued to SOE, where she joined the ranks of women whose love for France had brought them together toward the hour of flight.

Noor-Un-Nisa Inayat Khan, to be known from that hour forward as agent Paulette, was soft-spoken and almost painfully shy, in spite of her exotic beauty and slightness of stature. Though having failed during the mock interrogations, Noor was recruited as a much-needed wireless operator—called a *pianist*—because of her earlier training in Morse school in the WAAF, as well as her exceptional French. The irony would not be lost on these newly trained agents, most surely not those of French background anyway, that the history of those dots (dits) and dashes (dahs) of the Morse Code from almost one hundred years before was based on the word PARIS. The combination of dits and dahs for the five letters of PARIS (34 units) set the timing for sending and receiving messages. Noor's ability to rapidly tap signals was her strength as an agent. It was also this individual touch that could reveal an imposter was sending a message and that a source had been compromised. Would Noor have been pacified by this history of code sending during her schooling? Or now, as she headed toward Paris and into the heart of war, armed with code tapping equipment that would be her demise if discovered?

Though not popularly accepted overall, having always been a loner, Noor nevertheless managed to maintain an attitude of selflessness and accountability. Due to the failure of an earlier scheduled departure, Noor joined Cicely and Diana, along with a male agent, on the night of June 16th. Each agent's packet included a few white tablets, some to stay awake or to fall asleep, and one "L" (lethal) pill, a cyanide tablet to be taken only under the most extreme circumstances.

As a wireless operator, Noor was also given the crystals for her transmitter to complete her existence as agent Paulette.

Cicely Margot Gordon Lefort, to be known from that hour forward as agent Alice, was about to leave her past roles as nurse, gentlewoman, and wife of a French doctor forever. Perhaps Cicely's final hours of preparation for this night of leave included a farewell to Kitty under a pretense of travel to Wales. In spite of her commitment to return to France, Cicely must have had qualms about one more exit from the country of her birth, especially since her arrival in France would be in the midst of war. With her husband in Paris, a husband she must no longer acknowledge, the prospect of returning to the country which held her loyalty would draw Cicely forward into her new existence. The necessary secrecy surely added tension to the anticipation. Not one word about her mission could be uttered to Alix, or Franklin, or Kitty, or anyone else she knew.

Once back in France, would Cicely, now agent Alice, be able to resist the desire to follow the threads of her previous life—to walk through her own doorway in Paris, to step into her kitchen and peer into her closets and look out her window onto Avenue Bosquet, to touch her books and linens and pillows, to sit at the table where she took her tea, to return to her bedroom, to see her husband just once more, to regain her life, if only for a few moments? Would Alice in fact be so lucky as to be assigned to the Prosper Network operating out of Paris? Hidden away some place discreet was her packet of magic white tablets; tricks to avoid going down an *Alice in Wonderland* rabbit hole. How appropriate was her name for the adventure that lay ahead of her!

The day of her arrival back on the soil of France would be the 19th anniversary of her marriage to Alix. Could the ties to husband

and home have been on Cicely's mind as she was strapped into the plane that night, or was time lost in the excitement and fear of upheaval?

When the moment arrived, the recruits walked through the moonlit airfield where they clambered aboard the waiting Lysanders in a double flight arrangement, no longer Diana, Noor, Cicely, but now agents Paulette, Madeleine, Alice.

CL: Good. Good! Keep going. You have momentum.

# AIRFIELDS OF LAVENDER

McCairns (pilot for June 16-17 double flight), Verity, Pickard,
Vaughan-Fowler, Rymills (pilot for June 16/17 double flight), with
Verity's aeroplane MA-J "Jiminy Cricket."
*McCairns Collection, Tangmere Military Aviation Museum*

**FRANK ERNEST "BUNNY" RYMILLS,** the pilot for Cicely's flight, had flown with Royal Air Force (RAF) since June 1939. The run that night with Alice and the other agents was one in a string of 65 operations he flew without a break. The plane preferred for SOE operatives was the Westland Lysander, designed specifically for navigating small landing fields, flying below radar at slow speed without stalling, and providing a clear view forward for the pilot. Rymills specialized in takeoffs and landings from rough fields such as Vieux Briollay, the location where Cicely and the male agent aboard his Lysander were to be met by local organizer Henri Déricourt. SOE's intention to make their agents appear unglamorous made its mark on Cicely. Rymills later reported that she looked like a pastor's wife.

Perhaps Cicely's calm manner rattled him, for in spite of his many years of experience he accidentally left his radio transmitter on as they flew over the Channel and entered occupied territory above the moonlit French countryside. His cordial conversation with Cicely could be heard by Noor, Diana, and the pilot on the companion plane of this double flight, as well as by any Germans who might have happened to find their frequency. Cicely, with a soft-spoken demeanor belying the danger of the excursion—likely in a state of disbelief to be at long last back over France—asked the names of the villages below. The local landmarks described by Rymills could have exposed the secret location of their rendezvous with Déricourt.

Henri Déricourt had been organizing receptions for SOE agents arriving in France, and seeking suitable farm fields as landing grounds since January 1943, about the same time that Cicely, Noor, and Diana were recruited by SOE to work undercover in France. The agents on the two Lysanders that flew into France the night of June 16 were only four of the 67 agents whose transport Déricourt would arrange over the months of 1943.

Luckily, this night of their double flights, each agent's urgent scramble down the ladders attached to the side of the Lysander, landing at last with both feet in France, was achieved without any unfortunate happenstance. One of the agents on the ground waiting to return to England, Jack Agazarian, climbed up into the open passenger compartment of the plane, behind the pilot's cockpit, for his reentry and debriefing which would take place once they arrived safely back at Tangmere. Having been a wire operator himself, Agazarian understood the danger that any hesitation might cause. Quick movement was paramount. The engine was kept running on the ground and only two or three minutes separated landing and takeoff.

Even at an age twenty years more advanced than the other agents involved in this dual Lysander drop-off that night, Cicely rushed along and jumped on an awaiting bicycle for the seven-mile ride in the night to the village of Angers. From there, she and her compatriots would go by train to their assigned locations. Her mind must have raced as rapidly as her heart and her legs.

Imagine the scent of an early June morning, now the anniversary of her wedding. Even in time of war, a secluded field must have harbored the familiar clicks and chatter of insects and night creatures, and the ghost fragrance of lavender. The nostalgic sounds and smells of home must have seemed as painful as they were wonderful. But there was no time to reminisce. Every minute of exposure increased the chance of disaster.

Once they arrived in Angers, Diana's train took her to eastern France. where she was based out of a remote château. Much to Cicely's delight, she and Noor traveled by rail to Paris. What complicated emotions Cicely must have felt. Paris. So known and experienced and near to everything that mattered to her. Paris. Avenue Bosquet. Alix. How Cicely must have fretted, for now with the remote possibility of seeing her husband, could she possibly manage to resist? Only hours into her mission, would she breach every security rule and take such a risk? If she had the great fortune of a moment with Alix, she never revealed it, nor did anyone wish to ask, perhaps wanting to respect a woman's dedication to her private cause.

As with any mission in war, what can be kept undercover is something for which to be thankful. All too soon, Cicely—now as agent Alice—was on a train heading south to Montélimar, assigned for her secret mission to meet with the leader of the Jockey circuit, Francis Cammaerts, code name Roger. It was Noor who remained in Paris, working with the Prosper network, the organization that Déricourt was most involved with.

By the time the four agents from the flight of June 17th were on their way to their respective networks, Rymills and his passenger,

Agazarian, had safely returned to England. When Maurice Buckmaster met with the returning agent, Agazarian expressed concern about Henri Déricourt's loyalty. But there was not enough evidence to support his suspicion, and Déricourt continued to organize the receptions for agents in France. Only a week later, Noor reported to SOE that three of the lead members of her Prosper network in Paris, whose receptions Déricourt had organized, had been arrested by the Gestapo.

CL: As I mentioned to you earlier, that Déricourt was a bad piece of business. Handsome, oh yes! Which can always win some favors, but too slick for my liking. (I may have been the "time-worn" lady in the field, but I could still recognize and appreciate good looks!) I had a bad feeling about him from the moment he received us. I feel justified to know that he was suspected by others, and that his reputation followed him all the way to 2007 and was confirmed with your Mrs. Riols's scorn.

Jack, now. He was what you'd call a keeper. Agazarian. Such a nice young man. And the only agent I knew whose wife was also working in the same circuit. Now that would have caused anxiety, indeed. He and Cammaerts had similar motivations to join SOE, both having already lost younger brothers as RAF pilots to the war effort. As you know, Jack was convinced that Henri was up to no good, and in our situation, that could be lethal, or worse, torturous. Unfortunately, for Jack, his return to England was not long lasting, and soon he was back on French soil. (I suppose that a return to his wife might have been influential, too.)

The wireless set belonging to one of the arrested agents was still in service. Whoever was operating it, and we couldn't be sure who it was, had arranged a meeting. Jack and another SOE officer flipped to see who would make the rendezvous. Jack lost the toss and arrived at the address, even though he was certain the meeting was a trap, and it was. He was instantly arrested. That kind of news the enemy was eager for us to hear, as warning, though it never stopped any of us from our mission. I don't know what happened to Jack after that, but obviously word about this abortive mission and loss of agents got around to many of us. It was a big deal, and a warning for agents to keep at high alert.

L: Agazarian's route (apparently the familiar Jack, to you) through the French prison system was similar to yours, Cicely. First to Avenue Foch for interrogation, then prison at Fresnes, and finally on to Flossenbürg concentration camp. Sadly, he was executed just about the same time that you, dear Cicely, also disappeared at Ravensbrück.

CL: Such a shame, to lose a good man like Jack Agazarian. I am indeed sorry to have to know that. But, please, tell me more about the charming Francis Cammaerts. I know a bit about all this, as during training in England, the women had a lot of time to talk—we realized later that sometimes our conversations were a test of our loyalty, but that did not worry us enough to stop our chatter. So, we conversed, and a lot of stories passed amongst us. Francis was one who received reasonable coverage. You must have more background to reinforce his story, yes?

L: Yes, I'd be happy to reinforce the lore of Cammaerts. Allow me to return to my reporting voice.

With the Prosper network of Paris in distress, following Jack's arrest and the others taken in by Déricourt, the success of the Jockey circuit in the Rhone Valley, operated by this Francis Cammaerts, became paramount.

As a conscientious objector at the outset of World War II, Cammaerts seemed an unlikely recruit as a Special Operations Executive network organizer. With a Belgian poet father and a Shakespearean actress mother, Cammaerts's pacifist attitude caused Buckmaster's great doubts about him as agent material. But after his brother's death as an RAF pilot, Cammaerts changed his mind about being a conscientious objector, and he devoted himself to return to Buckmaster's operation.

In March, 1943, Cammaerts flew into a field to the west of Compiègne operating under the code name Roger, but the Donkeyman network he worked with was infiltrated by the Gestapo, in particular an agent named Hugo Bleicher of Abwehr. When it was realized that Bleicher's apartment was right next to Henri Déricourt's, suspicions increased to the likelihood that Déricourt was a double agent, as well.

Cammaerts set up the new organization named Jockey, radiating out of Lyon in southeast France. Because of Jockey's activity and success, Cammaerts asked for more agents. It was this need that brought the call to SOE headquarters for a new agent.

CL: A pause in the action, please! That call for a new agent was what propelled me back to France. Oh my, I do apologize for the interjection, but it's so exciting to feel like I'm back in the heart of it all, albeit this time around I have the advantage of not being fatigued and ill, as I was back then. I had arrived, Agent Alice, to work in Montélimar as Cammaerts's principal courier.

L: I understand your sigh, dear Cicely. This immersion must be overwhelming for you. But let's continue with Francis. He seems so present right now, I don't want to lose this thread. Here we go.

Cammaerts, called *le grand diable anglais*—the great English devil— by the local farmers because of his 6'4" stride and unmistakable British appearance, depended on Alice to transfer messages between him and other members of Jockey circuit. The range of this network extended from Lyons to the Mediterranean to the Italian and Swiss borders.

By D-Day, Cammaerts's Jockey circuit incorporated up to 10,000 fighters, each with fierce loyalty and respect for Roger—Colonel Roger by then—as the network leader. Cammaerts never stayed in the same place more than two nights but always knew where his agents were and how to get in touch with them. Contacts to him were made only by a transfer of messages and passwords. For a while, Alice was that messenger.

CL: That's right. I had been one of only a few agents who *did* know where he was. I do appreciate this "fresh" perspective, looking back over my past with such a global view. Cammaerts did strike a distinguished pose, and I was so honored to serve with him. Some of this news was tidbits that I was able to gather along the twisted path through French prison system and on into Germany, but I dare say there are some advantages to this removed storytelling.

L: Here's something that might surprise you, Cicely. Francis Cammaerts actually wrote to me. Of course it was once again only because of René Jamois's diligent work and concerted effort to assist us. (That would be to assist you and me. I feel as if we are both on this journey of discovery together.) This connection goes back to the year 2003. I'll just put it out here the way it unfolded, starting with this August 29, 2003 letter from René:

> I got more information from Mme Dumont about Francis Cammaerts. He was born in 1916 to a Belgian father and English mother. He was a principal in an English school. He was sent to southeastern France in March 1943 to organize a Résistance network of the utmost importance in anticipation of the landing of the Allied troops in Provence in August 1944. He was arrested in August 1944 but he could escape a few days later.
>
> I'll get in touch with Francis Cammaerts and go to see him next October or November.

L: December 12, 2003, I received another letter from René:

> Here are our Season Greetings for all our dear friends in the States... and some more information about Cicely Lefort.
>
> Two weeks ago we went to Le Pouget about 100 miles from Le Pontet to meet with Francis Cammaerts, the chief of the Jockey intelligence network in the south-east of France...
>
> We were heartily welcomed by what I called an 'out of ordinary' gentleman. He's of English origin but speaks a good French. A 87 year-old, tall (6 feet) and thin man with a moustache. Very typical British with a good sense of humour.
>
> We questioned him about Cicely and he told us: "Cicely arrived in 1943 and I didn't see her for a long time. Fewer contacts meant more security for the network.

*I gave her various missions, collections of information to be sent secretly to London, looking for dropping grounds for supplying arms and explosives, courier, etc."*

He went on. *"Cicely was very shy and I think too frail for this hard work she very courageously carried out. I advised her to be extremely careful. SOE made a risky choice to send her to France. She would have made a good worker in the Intelligence services in England, but I'm sure she insisted to come because she hoped to see her husband again. Anyway, I think she didn't see him. SOE security rules were very strict. When I saw that she was rather exhausted I asked SOE to take her back to England, but it was too late."*

Then Francis Cammaerts explained to us the role of his network. *It was mainly to get information about the German troops and military installation in the south-east of France because the Allied forces were planning a second landing in France on the Mediterranean coast after the June 6, 1944 landing on the Channel in Normandy.*

Francis remembered: *"I sent a message giving the state of the coast defenses and the best and more secure itineraries for the armies. I said that 7 days after the landing the troops would be 150 miles inside the country. In London, they thought I was getting crazy because they suffered fierce battles for a few miles in Normandy. They sent three officers (French, British and U.S.) to test my mental health! We travelled through the region and met very few German troops. The second landing took place on August 15 and my 'prediction' was right."*

Francis Cammaerts insisted to say that the merit of the work he organized was not his but that of all the courageous men and women who worked very dangerously inside the network and that he has the most grateful thoughts for Cicely and everybody.

We left him, very moved and impressed to have met with the gentleman.

L: That's some good first-hand information, isn't it Cicely? I hope you don't take offense to increasing references, shall I say concern, for your well-being, perhaps not among the strongest, youngest, or healthiest agents. However, as noted with Noor and others, there were multiple reasons that citizens chose to join the war effort, and being of good faith and loyal to the Allies, I suppose that feeling ill would not seem reason enough to desist.

I wrote to Francis Cammaerts soon after this, telling him about my interest and relationship to you. He wrote a postcard, reiterating his perception of your fragile state just before your capture, and of his gratitude to you for your dedication to the Jockey network. He welcomed me to visit him the next time I get to France!

But within a few months of receiving his message, René wrote with the news that Mr. Cammaerts has died.

CL: Francis died? But he was so tall and strong!

Oh my, yes. Time does go quickly by. Of course, he did die, finally, of age, yes? Dear me, this time warp really confuses my perspective.

L: And it was not too long after this that David Murphy, the scholar from Trinity College in Dublin, contacted me again. He had been to London and made copies of all of your SOE papers. He said he would send me copies.

"They are grim, and include eye witness accounts of Cicely's arrival at Ravensbrück and indications of the surgery for cancer," David wrote.

I was anxious to receive this file, anticipating the palimpsest layer of understanding it would add. As things turned out, this English file, when mixed in with your French dossier, exposed and explained much. In a literary sense, I feel it's fitting to say that the arrival of your English file deconstructs, in many ways, your French dossier. No, this has not been a simple story to tell. But well worth it, dear Cicely, well worth it.

In the meantime, I had already compiled a section about SOE agents' work, once you all were settled in your mission. May I?

CL: By all means. At this point I'd like very little break in the rhythm. Let's just keep pounding the keys and get it all out. What shall we name this?

# III. LA VIE D'ESPIONNAGE

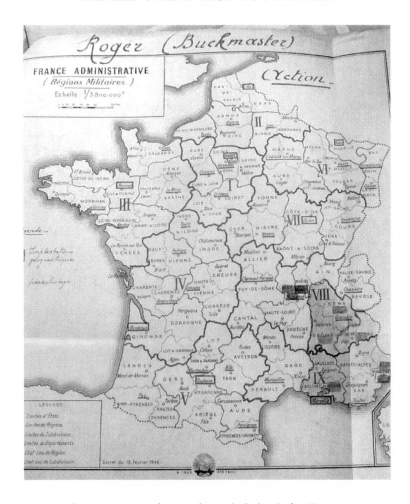

Buckmaster's map of networks, included in Lefort Dossier at
Ministry of Defense.
*Elizabeth Sloan*

# LIFE AS SPIES

Members of the Maquis in La Trésorerie, 1944.
Library and Archives Canada/Department of
*National Defence fonds/PA-166396*

**FOR THREE FEMALE BRITISH SOE AGENTS** dropped into France on a moon-spun night of June 16-17 in 1943—Cicely Lefort, Noor Inayat Khan, and Diana Rowden—the future would not be bright. None will survive, but eventually their stories will be told through others who did live to tell, and future generations who care to bear witness.

Because so much activity had been focused in the north of France with Operation Overlord gaining momentum in preparation for the Normandy D-Day Invasion, British supplies of ammunition and SOE support to the Vichy region of southern France had taken a lower priority, making the task of those involved with Résistance even more difficult. Even so, London put out orders to increase sabotage and create distraction in the south of France. An air drop of long awaited supplies was to be delivered.

For Cicely Lefort, courier work as Alice quickly absorbed each day and night. Day was the time to seek secure shelter away from illuminated spaces. Night was the time to move across the countryside under cover of shadows and darkness.

Now fully immersed in undercover ground operations, Alice was put in charge of bringing the plane in over the drop zone, substantially increasing the danger of her arrest. Alice carried the principal light on the ground to help the pilot locate the drop zone. Only weeks had passed since the Lysander that carried Cicely—soon to be known as Alice—had circled that northern field of Vieux Briollay, located the line of handheld lights or low-burning bonfires that showed the path, and securely sent her on the journey that led to this moment in another field, in southern France, with Alice now lighting the way.

The plane circled, dipped lower, circled once more, and sped off, so quickly gone, even the reception network wondered what had taken place. Lately, too much suspicious activity had been noticed by the Germans, who were now closing in on Jockey circuit. The line of destruction—mainly train derailments—that agents Roger and Alice had organized made them premium targets of the Gestapo.

Would these agents on the ground beneath the circling plane remain wholeheartedly dedicated to resistance, or would weariness and the hour by hour increase of likely capture take their toll, until the agents wished they were on the plane, heading back to England?

The disappointed reception committee members quickly took cover and dispersed separately into the shadows and hedgerows. Accomplices reconnected at a safe-house where they spent the next hours and days gathered around a battered kitchen table, anxious hands intermittently fingering their short-wave radio dial bringing in a scratchy reception, every member focused especially on listening to the nightly broadcast by the British Broadcasting Corporation over the BBC network and waiting for the pre-arranged encoded message that another drop would be attempted.

Since 1940, the BBC had been committed to the war effort through frequent broadcasts of a ridiculous string of phrases, repeated word for word, some of which were meaningless, but others containing coded messages from the British-based Allies to partisan operatives: "The goat next door has eaten grandfather's vest," or "There's a cow sleeping on the couch." In this case, the reception committee waited for a color to be added, such as a red vest or a brown cow, indicating that immediate action was necessary, and setting into motion the scramble to round up carts and get word out for agents to make their way to a designated landing field.

Within days, the addition of a "red vest" forecast the arrival of new supplies that would be dropped and successfully gathered, with the intention to continue the build up of Operation Overlord. The Lyon railway and power lines, as well as the hydro-electric station, were delegated as the target of destruction, in an attempt to reduce the production of German aircraft.

Noor Inayat Khan, as agent Madeleine, had been working her way around Paris during the months that Alice maneuvered her way throughout the Rhône Valley. In some ways it must have seemed surreal to be back in the city where she'd been a student at the Sorbonne during her schoolgirl days. Perhaps the familiarity of Madeleine's locale caused her to be so casual as to forget about the need for discretion when passing on information and making contacts. A couple close calls—transmission schedules aborted by sightings of SS on location, and a German officer walking by as she attempted to loop the radio aerial on to a tree branch—nearly gave her position away within the first couple weeks of her mission.

Her situation was all the more precarious, due to the added responsibility of operating the radio to send coded messages back to London headquarters, a duty requiring constant relocation, staying in each place of transmission for no more than thirty minutes, quickly dismantling the equipment, and discreetly moving out.

All these precautions could not guarantee anonymity. Indeed, when Madeleine passed through the neighborhood of Suresnes, where she had lived before the war, an acquaintance recognized her and called out her name.

"Noor Inayat!"

For that moment, suddenly having to think once more of herself as Noor, and urgently needing to forget she was agent Madeleine, she tried earnestly to answer the questions of where she'd been—as Noor—since the war began, and what she had been doing with her life, all without giving away her work as a secret agent. In spite of this attempt, the neighbor and she finally realized that they were both involved with a campaign of resistance, much to their mutual relief.

It was during those first critical weeks after Noor's mid-June arrival that she, as Madeleine, had to send the troubled message about the near collapse of the Prosper circuit due to the arrest of a number of agents, especially those whose arrival had been organized by Henri Déricourt. Ironically, however, Déricourt must have taken a liking to Madeleine—perhaps cared for her enough to risk his own duplicitous intentions—for he tried a number of times to convince her to return to London, but each time the clandestine SOE landings had to be canceled.

The full moon necessary for flights to and from France came and went, and yet another month passed. In the meantime, the Germans had the fortune of discovering some incriminating papers at a letterbox where Madeleine had briefly stayed. Papers that identified her elusive code-name. They now realized for the first time that the radio operator working in Paris was not a man, as they had suspected, but a woman named Madeleine. An intensive search for her was initiated, including descriptive leaflets tacked onto posts and the lure of a bounty as motivation to turn her in.

In spite of the way Vera Atkins trained female agents to appear nondescript, Noor's natural wiles and exotic beauty had up to this point been put to good use. But her good luck with good looks, as Madeleine, would not last.

The third agent to arrive in France the same June night as Cicely and Noor was Diana Rowden, agent Paulette. It is possible that Diana's route as a spy with the Acrobat Network crossed the paths of Noor and Cicely, for she traveled frequently between Marseille, Lyon, and Paris. It's even possible that she delivered messages directly to Cicely, as their circuits intersected around Lyon. This must have provided a moment of warmth through an unexpected reconnection with another agent who had shared the entry into France on that June night.

Diana's daily life would have been quite similar to Cicely's, since both agents covered large territories and worked across the countryside, as opposed to Noor's work focused in Paris. Diana's time working undercover would last just one month longer than that of Cicely and Noor. And yet, of this trio, Diana would be the agent held for the shortest time—and the first one to die.

Agent Paulette's first assignment in France bordered on luxury. Partly due to the slight British accent detectable in her otherwise impeccable French, she was headquartered in a medieval castle, the Château Andelot, located in a secluded section of Vichy France not far from the Swiss border. Also housed here was the leader of her network, as well as his wireless operator, who had an even more detectable English accent.

From this safe house, Paulette moved across the countryside, usually by bicycle or by train, where no doubt her natural birdlike features helped her avoid attention. As happened to most agents, detection was a constant threat, but Paulette was clever and quick enough to slip out of many a dangerous situation.

As she became more involved and proficient in the cause of espionage, Paulette's travels took her deeper into the mountainous regions, whereupon she, like Alice, became responsible for a number of successful clandestine drops. One of the most important missions was the drop of explosives and arms that led to the sabotage of the Peugeot factory, setting the German Army back three months in their production of war tanks.

By September of 1943, three months into Paulette's mission, the leader of her circuit was captured, and the key backup agent began to suspect that a double-agent had infiltrated their network. SOE agents in the field were advised to lie low. Paulette moved from the château and took up residence with a family who operated a café, at times even serving the patrons, while taking on the role of a French mademoiselle doing her part to wait out the war.

Even so, the agent Paulette was shortly arrested, in mid-November of 1943, on suspicion of helping the Résistance. That the cafe where she waited tables was near the Swiss border worked in her favor, though, as her stilted accent might have been attributed to the many renters who tended to move across the border to work. The Gestapo let her go, never aware that they had captured the very agent most wanted because of her involvement with successful drops of supplies that had led to much destruction in the area.

A few weeks later, Paulette moved on again, feeling the pull to get back into operation, to make contacts again with London and the local Résistance workers. Moving to the Clairvaux region, Paulette took on yet another disguise, this time changing her name to Marcelle, initiating new hair and clothing styles. Marcelle's story was that she was a cousin to the family who operated a local sawmill, and she had come to stay with them to regain strength after her long illness.

As an agent, Marcelle again became active with resistance, organizing supply drops and relaying messages. Her involvement became all the more crucial, due to the breakup of the Prosper network, the circuit that Noor worked with in Paris. Much-needed agents were requested, and London managed to send one man to assist Marcelle and her network.

The man SOE sent, and the others with him, landed to a Déricourt-arranged reception. Though these newly arrived agents managed to escape immediate defeat, they were trailed on the train to Paris and arrested on arrival there, adding credence to the suspicion among SOE that Déricourt was at least a double agent. (It would be the pilot of Cicely's Lysander, Bunny Rymills, who would write *Henri Déricourt: Double or Triple Agent* after the war, referencing from his first hand witness perspective.)

CL: I'm stunned. Such investigative work! I did not know so much of this, as you must realize, though some of the information had circulated as rumors. I'm sure many of our agents were aware of the details you relate (and we know that Mrs. Riols was able to enlighten you to some of the clandestine work, such as those silly radio announcements as a code to pass information.) Again, looking back on it all in one package, as you've clearly provided, I see why there is so much intrigue from those who never lived it. In fact, even knowing the path, I do believe I would not have traded the adventure, even if I could have been offered a longer life. I'll be so bold as to say, had I not lived this life (and died this death), dear Lizzie, you would not have taken an interest in me or my world, and I would truly have died with no reminder or purpose.

You, my Lizzie, are as dependable as those 'Lizzies' that stayed the course through the moonlit nights. I just now remembered our affectionate name for the Lysanders that safely delivered me, and so many other agents, into the darkened fields of war! You also have brought me to a better understanding of the worthwhile work we did in the face of death, and the collective meaning of our united front. *Merci, mon amie, merci.*

L: I'm relieved to know that my revelations of your undercover work provide some sense of closure, or at least perhaps acceptance. You're right, on many counts, my dear "cousin" (please, for simplicity sake). I believe, sadly, that what you say is true—about your life and death having universal meaning, because of the war.

It is also sad, but true, that even though in the end, your death (by disappearance) was not a number counted, your flight on a 'Lizzie" was. The after-war statistics show that the time honored Lysanders delivered 293 agents, right down to the exact count, into the European field of war.

It seems fair to say that Diana, Noor, and you can claim that final wrap of the digit 3. Sadly, however, not one of you can be counted in 410 recovered agents, though both you and Noor apparently were intended for a call back flight.

Forgive me, Cicely. I recall that indeed, the heartbreaking account of your death is recorded as a number, in that there were 13 female SOE agents from F Section who did not return from war. Again, it appears that you three once very lively ladies can claim that final number of the digit 3.

But enough about Numerology. Let's move along.

You know, I did indeed ask Mrs. Riols if she had the chance, would she do it again? Without hesitation, though, she said, "No! No, but we were young!"

And Vera Atkins, your rigorous Intelligence Officer for F Section. What can you say about her, Cicely?

CL: She was tough on us. Had to be. (She did have that rugged Romanian personal constitution as well.) It was for our own good. For the good of the entire war, for if one of us fell, many more went down, too. But she was also like a mother hen, always taking us under her protective wing. She was not just concerned that operations would be arrested. She deeply cared for each one of us, and felt responsible for our safety and our return, though many of her agents did not return. That must have been very hard on her, sending us out in to the center of the war zone, knowing…well, knowing what we all came to know. The average time for an agent to operate before being captured was only six months. I lasted only on the short side of that statistic.

I should have been more careful.

L: Yes, it is true that Vera did care. You will find out just how much, as we talk a little further. Shall we, then? I can tell you what I have learned about the arrests. I might have taken some liberties with how I envisioned your capture, but based on family interviews and the memoirs of those who did survive, I think I'm close. There's no avoiding it now.

# ARRESTED

Truffe au Nougat package from Montélimar.
*Elizabeth Sloan*

**MONTÉLIMAR IN THE AUTUMN OF 1943** was beginning to see the first effects of what was to come in the year to follow. Allied planning for the European front focused on the invasion in northern France (code Operation Overlord), while in Sicily, an assault on the French Mediterranean (code Operation Anvil) was being developed in a collaborative effort. It would be months before these attacks were set in motion. However, in the meantime, the strategically located valley of Montélimar had already become a hub of resistance activity.

Raymond Daujat, the resistance leader involved with both Cammaerts's and Cicely's Jockey circuit in Montélimar, lived in a gated whitewashed house on the edge of the town. The German investigations at this time focused on the location of agents Roger and Alice because of the extensive destruction these agents were responsible for. Roger was aware of the intensified search and warned Alice to keep her distance from the headquarters at Daujat's villa, but agent Alice must have been too weary to heed the caution.

Imagine the temptation to experience just one secure night inside the walls of a house that would feel like a home; one night's sleep in a real bed with a soft pillow to allow dreams of a life so far removed as to seem merely a delusion. Imagine the mid-September night's air, crisp off the mountains with wisps of clouds hovering above the valley. The damp dirt smell of leaves. The rustle of rabbits and voles escorting Alice up the path and through the pillared gate to Daujat's door, as if she were arriving by invitation for a party. The sounds of distant explosions of sabotage setting an almost celebratory mood. Daujat would be surprised, perhaps alarmed, to open his door to the middle-aged and no doubt exhausted Alice.

If only Roger's plea to SOE for Alice's return to England had gotten through. Even as she stood upon this safe-house door stoop, the message for her removal was on its way, or had already arrived to Buckmaster. But even if Alice were aware of the approaching end to her assignment, it would have been in character for her to carry on with the mission, delving as diligently as possible until the moment of departure.

If only she could fulfill this one much needed rest. One tranquil night was all she asked.

In spite of the risk, surely Daujat could not deny her. Would a meager meal of stew be served? The stub from a week-old but still tasty baguette offered? A prized bottle of Bordeaux brought up from the cellar to sip while tales were shared of espionage, or perhaps memories of lives long behind them, spoken in whispers as if kept from the shadows beyond the window panes?

Sleep would come to her, with hours enough to go deep, past the dream stage, into oblivion, letting go of the scramble of messages yet to be delivered, the hesitation, the fear.

Then, pounding. Banging on the villa door, as loud as a panzer, scraping Alice up from the depth of her sleep. Raymond Daujat would have jumped from his bed, the moment of his greatest dread crashing down on his own sleep-confused mind. Had he called out in an urgent whisper? *Alice, attendez vous. Immediatement.* Would he have shown her a place to hide, just in case, before they had pushed the cork back in the carafe and retired for the night? There was not time for planning an escape.

Daujat opened his door as the Gestapo shoved past him. It would be up to Alice to hide. Daujat was arrested, but was allowed a quick stop in the bathroom. As the Gestapo rampaged through the house in search of Alice, Daujat managed to scramble from the bathroom window and escape through the trees.

The cellar, of course! Alice hurried below and squeezed beneath some floorboards, perhaps a space she had noticed when the wine had been retrieved only a few hours earlier.

Did she breathe too loudly? Did she move without realizing it, make some slight scratching noise with her elbow or knee? Did the pounding of her heart betray her? Before she had a chance to calm down from the terror of hiding, she was roughly hauled out of the cellar, handcuffed, arrested, shoved out the door, down the steps, and into a car with its engine still running.

It was the beginning of the end for this woman known as agent Alice.

CL: It was foolish of me to go to Dajaut's door. *Je le regrette beaucoup.* That bit about the wine, nice idea, but not so much true. The scene you put us in was, indeed, what I would have liked to experience. What warm-blooded person wouldn't at that point? Just a touch of real life again! But, no, that was not to be. Not ever. To think, though, that I put Raymond in such danger, for my selfish need. Another regret: Alain, another member of the local resistance movement, was hidden in the villa this very same night. I believe he, too, was able to escape, for which I am most grateful.

L: Ah yes, you're right, Cicely. René did make a note about this man, Alain. His real name was Paul Reynaud, and here, yes, here I have a letter in fact that Mr. Reynaud wrote all the years later, on September 26, 1951, recommending that you be awarded the Legion of Honor, for which you were. And you know, your dear husband was part of this campaign to honor your sacrifice. You were, you are indeed, very much loved and respected. But back to that awful night at Daujat's villa. Cammaerts reflected on your capture, too, when René and he had their visit. He told René:

> A tragic example of Cicely's frailty. When the German Gestapo knocked at the door of Raymond Daujat in Montélimar, she'd enough time to escape through the back yard and fly away. Instead she only thought to take shelter in the coal cellar where they found her and arrested her. Raymond Daujat jumped through a narrow window and escaped. He was killed a few months later during a sabotage mission.

L: Cicely, there is also mention of an incriminating piece of paper in your possession. Another hint of this will be revealed much later.

CL: I had heard that Raymond Daujat died not too long after, but I did not know what actually happened. Can you tell me?

L: Yes, in fact I can. You see, even now, in my current time and place, others still find your story, and the story of so many other war victims, important to tell and remember.

There is another British historian who wrote to me only recently, wanting to write a brief biography about each of the female SOE agents who went to France. He wondered what I could tell him about you. Well, tell him I did! And the exchange has been a mutual gift. This Paul McCue revealed that Raymond Daujat died, ironically, as a result of his quite successful sabotage mission, the one Cammaerts referred to.

It was December 9, 1943 (less than three months after your arrest), a nighttime mission to blow up a railway south of Montélimar. You probably know the area from your time there, Cicely. Of all crazy things, just as the rails were destroyed, a train arrived, derailed, and struck Daujat dead.

CL: Tragedy, over and over again. And not the least, nor the last of disastrous consequences.

You've told about my arrest, Lizzie. I suppose you can also tell about Noor and Diana's captures. This is awful to hear, but necessary and important, I know.

I'm listening.

On October 13, only three days after Cicely's arrest as agent Alice, Noor, as agent Madeleine, too, was captured when she was betrayed by an acquaintance who let a Gestapo agent into her flat. Madeleine returned from an errand and unsuspectingly walked into the trap. She ferociously tried to fight her way out. A back-up of Gestapo officers was called in to assist in the arrest of this one slightly built agent. Madeleine was hauled to 84 Avenue Foch, to the 5th floor holding cells where the Gestapo interrogated SOE agents, and where she, too, would be pushed to her limits to maintain silence under all circumstances, especially for the first crucial 48 hours.

With their covers compromised, Cicely and Noor had been arrested. Not long after their arrests, Marcelle, soon to regard herself as Diana once again, was also arrested. On November 17, 1943, agent Marcelle awaited the arrival of the new agent. When he appeared, the introduction was filled with excitement of supplies and messages the agent had delivered. He then went away to retrieve his suitcase, which he said he had left behind. Marcelle went with him and told him about the circuit's work and other details necessary for his activity in the area. The rest of the morning and afternoon the agents went on separately about their work.

Meanwhile, Cuthbert, the network leader, returned to the sawmill and was beginning to consider his intuition about this new agent. Something about his vagueness of activity in London, something about the questions he asked, made Cuthbert uneasy. When the new agent returned that evening, the leader intended to question him.

Dinners at the sawmill were a time for all to convene, and the new agent walked Marcelle up the path to the villa. She did not know that he was flashing a light behind him to show his location, all the way up the road. Inside, the Madame of the family prepared dinner, chatting with Cuthbert while they waited for others to arrive.

Marcelle and the new agent entered the house. Almost immediately, the scream of tires interrupted the calm, and a group of Gestapo agents broke down the door. The intrusion overwhelmed the Madame. She stood helplessly aside as Cuthbert and Marcelle were dragged along with the new agent into the waiting cars. The three agents were taken to the local *polizeistation* and delivered to separate cells. Cuthbert was tortured in an attempt to find where the transmitter was hidden. Marcelle, perhaps thinking of herself as Diana again, heard his cries of pain through the walls, but Cuthbert held out, revealing nothing.

Another agent in the network heard of the arrests, warned others to disperse and bravely came to the house a short while later to remove the radio transmitter, just in time. The new agent who was arrested alongside Marcelle and Cuthbert, but only as a means to keep his cover, soon also returned to the house in search of the transmitter. Cuthbert's earlier suspicion was well founded. This new agent was not the one sent from London after all, but was an impostor, a Frenchman in the pay of the Germans, who had taken on the clothes and information of the real SOE agent, one of the two men who had been arrested when they arrived in Paris by train.

It seemed that Pétain's warning, back in 1940, not to trust anyone, held much truth. SOE agents who put their lives on the line in good faith with their compatriots—particularly the vulnerable aspect of dropping into enemy territory to behave as if they belonged there—would be done in by their own lack of imagination to suspect even those closest to them. Diana was about to be introduced to the depths these deceptions took.

CL: Pétain. *Pthewww*! I spit on him. He handed France over to Germany. I suppose it's fair to say that this outrageous surrender he promoted is the reason I had to take such an abrupt leave from my husband and my home. Vichy collaborator! Talk about double crossers. Alix could barely hear the name without getting worked up into a fury, and you might imagine that Alix was not a man of anger. Self-serving Pétain, only looking out for himself. He could switch the lapel pin to his party of favor so quickly (meaning whichever one was in his best interest), it would make your head spin. Now there's another "what if," if you're looking for one. "What if Pétain had not been a collaborator!" But that will get me nowhere, so I must give it up.

You are prepared to provide more story, yes, Lizzie? And poor Diana. She was caught up in the often inescapable circumstances of war, leading to the torture of her leader and the eventual departure of them both from this earth.

By now, this is history, so we might as well put it out there. I'm not saying I like it.

I think you should title this next part "Departures."

L: And so I shall, Cicely, so I shall.

# DEPARTURES

LEFORT  C. M. (A/S O. W.A.A.F.).      2.      MONTELIMAR
ALICE/TEACHER/Cec  M. LEGRAND.       ROGER/JOCKEY/Comm  ts crot.

Left 16.6.43 by Lysander.
Courrier to ROGER.

19.9.43.  Roger announced ALICE arrested 16.9.43 at DAUJAT.

19.4.44  JACQUELINE thought she had been sent to Germany.

10.4.44.  From Roger dated 26.3.44.  Have been able to verify
          situation of ALICE who is in camp in Germany.

30.5.45  *[handwritten]* Alice dies in Ravensbruck

W.A.A.F. Casualty P/F.                     22666/A

                                           Buckmaster.

SOE memo addressing Alice's arrest.
*Dr. David Murphy*

**DIANA ROWDEN,** at one time known as agent Paulette, and finally as Mademoiselle Marcelle, was the last to be arrested of the three female agents who entered France on the night of June 17, but she will be the first to die.

Infiltration by Gestapo within resistance networks came from sources and in many forms. When Diana was transferred to Paris, to the Gestapo headquarters at 84 Avenue Foch, she was dismayed to discover that the network leader originally in charge of her circuit— captured months earlier, the man whom she had most trusted with her life—was now on good terms with the Gestapo. She saw him, unharmed and with Gestapo privileges, upon her arrival. Nevertheless, though tricked and demoralized, Diana held out and provided no information to her interrogators. Three weeks later, on December 5, she was transferred to Fresnes Prison, another thoroughfare for SOE agents to pass through, usually on their way to German concentration camps.

It wasn't until May of 1944 that Diana was sent to a German prison in Karlsruhe, where she survived in a crowded cell until early July when once again she was ordered to move out. It would be her last transfer.

This time, Diana Hope Rowden may indeed have had a moment of hope, for her belongings were returned to her, she was allowed to dress in her own clothes, and she was told she would be leaving. She was joined by three other SOE women agents. Any hope quickly dissipated when, after a journey by van and train with two members of the Gestapo, Wassmer and Ott, they arrived at Natzweiler-Struthof Concentration Camp. Suspicions rose, as Natzweiler was primarily a men's prison, increasing tension among the male prisoners when they saw the arrival of the four women and realized something must be about to happen.

The four women were separated and locked two to a cell, where they waited until after dark. Diana's companion was called out, and Diana was left alone, until she, too, was taken from the cell and led to a hospital block at the end of a path. Told that she would be given a typhus injection, she obediently lay on one of the eight cots. Most likely, death was immediate from a lethal dose of phenol. July 6, 1944, at age 29, Diana's life ended. Her body was tossed into the crematorium, along with those of the three agents who had just been murdered with her. The following day, on July 7, 1944, while Diana's death was still unknown to SOE and its resistance networks, SOE sent another agent into France.

Christine Granville, as agent Pauline, was to replace Cicely in Francis Cammaerts's still successful and crucial Jockey circuit. Her story, too, would have far-reaching impact. She would be the only one of these women connected by virtue of espionage and love for homeland to survive the war, though a tragic death would be her end as well.

Repercussions from D-Day continued, and with the expected arrival of Allies in the south of France, Roger was in need of reinforcements. While most of F section's agents in France came from England, Christine did not fit the usual profile. She was connected to the Algiers unit of SOE, and unlike the other two agents with French attachments so closely associated with Cicely, Christine came from Polish heritage. But like the three other agents with a love for their country of France, it was Christine's fierce devotion to Poland that drove her to defend the name of her homeland, at any cost.

Krystyna Gizycka was born to aristocratic parents. Her father was Count Skarbek, and her mother was a Goldfelder, of the wealthy Polish-Jewish banker family. Krystyna grew up to be an exceptional beauty. Though first married in 1938 at age 23, she was soon divorced and remarried, the second time to a writer twice as old as she. Krystyna Skarbek and her husband lived in Africa until 1939, when Germany invaded Poland. Krystyna's passion against the Nazis' invasion of her homeland held more power than her passion for marriage, and soon she was off to Hungary where she changed her name to *Christine Granville* and dedicated herself to the cause of resistance.

Christine had a gift for learning languages and an ability to debate eloquently, and her beauty and charm conquered many men. She used her assets for whatever end was necessary. Her impressive dossier included a number of narrow escapes and arrests, numerous frantic skiing trips across the Tatra Mountains to aid Polish prisoners, and some parachute training in Egypt. She provided information that informed and prepared Winston Churchill for the Soviet Union invasion of June 1941. The story goes that Christine even won the heart of a Gestapo guard dog who made an immediate switch of loyalty and remained with Christine for months of travel. These legendary escapades provided endurance and credibility for her to make her way through enemy country in the heart of the Nazi invasion in France. She joined

Cammaerts's Jockey circuit that summer of 1944.

Only one month after Christine, as agent Pauline, had joined the Jockey circuit—only three days after the Allied invasion on the southern coast of France—Roger and another agent were arrested. The combination of an air raid siren, a checkpoint, and possession of Résistance bank notes led to incarceration, harsh questioning, and intended disposal in a death cell. Roger had finally been trapped. There was little hope for his survival. His execution was scheduled to take place within hours of his capture.

But then Pauline heard about her leader's predicament.

With hopes of a German victory dwindling and Nazi nervousness about the threat of war crimes, blackmail had its virtues. Posing as both Roger's wife and the niece of the feared British Field Marshal Montgomery, Pauline wrote a statement clearing the local gendarmes in charge of Dignes prison where Roger was being held of collaborating with the Nazis. A bold and outrageous move indeed, but it worked. Finally, *La Milice française*, a fascist Vichy military group allowed Roger to escape with Pauline. Indeed, once again the life of the much admired Roger had been saved by his courier.

It must be wondered, if Cicely had not been captured—if Christine Granville had not been Cammaerts's chief assistant at that point in the war—would he, too, have perished?

CL: Yes, a fair enough "what if." What if Christine had not been in place of me, would Cammaerts have survived? Oh how I hate to admit this, but I dare say that he surely would not have. I was far too reserved, it is true. Christine was rare and brave indeed. Of course I had not met her, but word was circulating about this alarmingly beautiful and frightfully ingenious agent. I must say, when I got wind that she had taken over my post, I felt quite honored, as if I had anything to do with her ability, anyway.

Do you have something to add, Lizzie?

L: Yes, I do. I love the overlap of the history, the story, and the conversation I had with Mrs. Riols. So, come back to March, 2007, and my visit with her in Marley-le-roi. From my notes:

Late afternoon sunlight glimmered off the strand of pearls that Mrs. Riols wore. She shifted in her chair, crossing her arms as if a signal of achievement when I mentioned that Cicely worked for Francis Cammaerts, and then she recalled how Christine had rescued him.

"Back in London, all the agents and Buck were feeling sad and down. It was the night Cammaerts was to be executed. All night and that next morning we thought he was dead. Next day in London, in walked Cammaerts, cool as anything, as if he just got off work."

CL: Even in the most dire circumstances, I must chuckle. That was so "Roger." What I would have given to be able to witness that grand entry.

L: Would you like to hear what became of Christine after the war? She did survive, for a while anyway. I suppose if anyone could, it would be she.

CL: Absolutely, do tell.

L: Christine Granville's life as a spy exhilarated her, and she found life after the war tiresome and uninspiring. Floating from a job as sales clerk at Harrods to switchboard operator at India House in London, she seized the opportunity to be a stewardess on an ocean liner. And it might have been a good career move, but for a schizophrenic fellow employee who, like so many before him, was mesmerized with Christine's beauty. Not only was Christine uninterested in this man, but it's been hinted that she had an ongoing affair with a real catch, Ian Fleming, the author who created James Bond.

The rumor goes that Ian later based his first female 007 agent, Vesper Lynd in the movie *Casino Royale*, on this fiery woman. Be that completely true or not, it is not at all so far fetched. Drama and tragedy followed Christine to her death, when, in June of 1952, the rebuked and delusional suitor murdered her.

CL: Ian Fleming? James Bond? I'm sorry. I don't know what that means.

L: I keep forgetting. *Pardonnez-moi.* That was all later, after.... You probably don't even know who the dear child Anne Frank was, do you?

CL: I knew a lot of Anne's, of course. Annie, Anna, Ann. But a child? Anne Frank? No, that's not sounding familiar. I don't think our paths ever crossed. I suppose she became an unfortunate figure of the war as well, since you mention her even now. I'm not sure I'm up for hearing about that. I am feeling quite weary.

L: Shall I go on, where we left off, after Cammaerts's escape? Yes? All right, but I must warn you, the story keeps getting darker.

September 1944. Two months after Diana's death and Christine's entry into Jockey circuit as replacement for Cicely. Noor, too, had endured interrogations and prison for almost a year. Wassmer and Ott, the same two Gestapo men who had escorted Diana and the three agents who had arrived with her to their deaths at Natzweiler, now had charge of Noor with orders to deliver her to Dachau. Noor attempted twice to escape from prison when she was held in Paris at a building seized by the Nazis, 84 Avenue Foch. Once through a fifth floor bathroom window, and another time across the rooftops. She was thus considered a high risk prisoner and was moved to Pforzheim prison, where she was kept chained by hands to feet in solitary confinement. Even so, she managed to communicate with fellow political prisoners by scraping on metal dinner bowls and humming tunes.

And then it seemed her world might be returned. In a surreal twist of events, Noor was taken from Pforzheim and joined three other French Section agents, women she had known during SOE training.

The four agents, guarded by Wassmer and Ott, must have been hopeful when they were put in a reserved train compartment, allowed to smoke English cigarettes, to talk and laugh, and eat bread and sausage through the night hours of travel. When they got off the train just after midnight, September 12, they carried their luggage up the hill, perhaps only then realizing they had arrived at Dachau.

In the morning, a short walk to a sandy, bloodstained courtyard, became their final moments. Holding hands and kneeling, Noor, Yolande, Madeleine, and Eliane were each shot through the back of the head.

Or this, as accounts vary for many who were murdered: Noor's defiant attitude led to a more cruel ending, one that involved being stripped, beaten, chained, and shot, alone in her cell. But even then, not without shouting "*Liberté*" before her last breath left her.

L: Oh, the courage for Noor Inayat of poet-temperament. Once again, I'd like to interject a personal anecdote.

CL: Please, Lizzie, of course. I want to know about your life as much as you may want to know about mine. We are family, as the saying goes, so please do share. I care about you, too, you know. This mustn't all be about me.

L: Thank you. I appreciate that. I would like to tell you about a war experience my father had, before he was my father. His platoon was in Germany at the end of the war, and he went to Dachau soon after the "camps" were liberated. He wrote a letter home to his parents and it was printed in the town's paper. I have a copy of the article.

But first, Cicely, dear, I must insert another aside here. During "your time" of life, thank goodness for carbon paper. Were it not for that, there would be no record of your life and journey. Every paper I have regarding you is as a result of someone making a carbon copy while typing the original. Let me tell you, you would not recognize this world of "copy" we now inhabit. I can't even begin to explain to you how the world has progressed from mimeographs to Xerox copiers to computers.

Yes, I know, I know. Your puzzled look. (Oh for goodness sake, Cicely, America has had men literally walk on the moon.) Ah, that made your eyes open wide. It's true! Anyway, as I was saying, I also cannot count how many times I have made a *copy* of my father's letter about his experience at Dachau, and how many times I have come across even one of those copies in all my boxes and stacks of documents, every time thinking, "Oh I can find that when I want it, I have so many copies!" But now, for the absolute life of me, I cannot find one of those. So a respite is in order, while I search, furiously and quite absurdly.

While I'm looking (I remind myself of Mrs. Riols here, looking for her Pearl), let me also say that I realize I refer to you as 'Cicely dear,' as if you were a youth to my age. Indeed, I am now 15 years older than you were when you were...were murdered. Just as Anise Postel-Vinay referred to you as a young lady, we all seem locked in our own world of time, a situation which I find to be quite marvelous. Who cares about our ages? What matters is, well, you, and I, and all the others on this journey.

Oh look, I found a copy. (Such enthusiasm for what to follow is a very somber reflection.) Here now, my father's letter home:

> *One day I drove over to Dachau, the prison camp where so much slaughter took place. Don't for one minute think that the reports you heard about these places were propaganda. No reporter with the wildest imagination could conjure a picture of horror equal to these slaughter pens. They were terrible. At one place they had a sort of table built up with a big rock in the middle of it where they bashed small children's heads in and pitched them in a pile at one side. We gave some canned food to one little fellow about 30 or 35 years old, who was no more than skin and bones. He walked with a cane very feebly. The food we gave him could have been easily carried by a 10 year-old kid but this man could hardly shuffle along with it. All the time we were filling up the sack for him he sort of cried and sniffled and repeated over and over again in very broken English, "Thank you, thank you, thank you."*

CL: This was your father, you say? Oh my. That damn war (all wars!) affected so many lives. I'm sorry your father had to witness

that (but it is so very important that the world does know). I can't
begin to...no, I really can't think about such things.

L: Yes, you're right, so many lives. At one point earlier in the
war, Dad (I'll call him for the sake of convenience) had just jumped
off the back of a jeep when a land mine blew it up; a close call to my
never existing, to be sure.

After Germany, my dad was on a ship heading toward the
Pacific arena when Japan surrendered. His brother, Uncle Dick, was
a Prisoner of War in Japan, but he never spoke about it, ever. So you
see why it is so necessary for your story to be told. All right, forgive
my interruption. Let's get back on task to the departure, execution,
and memory of these brave British SOE agents.

October 1944. Noor: Dead, one month ago. Diana: Dead, three months.
Christine: working for the network, three months. Cicely: prisoner,
12 months.

Mrs. Cicely Lefort: no longer an aristocratic British woman with
a passion for horseback riding and sailing, married to a French
doctor and living in Paris. No longer a woman with hopes of
returning to any semblance of pre-war life. Even after interrogation
at prisons in Montélimar, Marseille, and Toulouse, Cicely held out.
No amount of contusions or breakage would bring forth useful
information for her persecutors, and Roger's Jockey circuit remained
intact. Truly, with the arrival of Christine, the network flourished.

L: Cicely? CICELY!

CL: I'm here. I'm here.

L: You're not fading on me, are you? I feel you pulling away.

CL: Hmmmm? No ma'am. I'll be fine. I'm just feeling run down, run over is more like it. This is hard. I'm so tired.

L: I think we both need a break. Put aside the reminiscence of war. Let's come back tomorrow. Rest now.

L: Good morning, Cicely. Rested? Good. This is going to be a big day. Are you ready? I'm not so sure I am either, but it's time.

CL: Now that I know what happened to my comrades, Noor, Diana, and Christina, I need to retrace my journey to hell, don't I?

L: I'm sorry, but yes, we do. I've prepared the work for you, so you can just listen. And no, it's not pretty.
Breathe. Again. God I hate this.

# NUMBERS

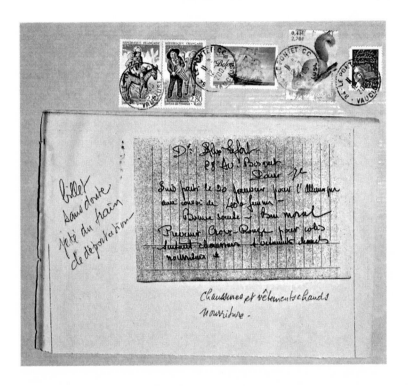

Note tossed from train to Ravensbrück, on envelope from Réne.
*Lefort family collection*

**STILL TO COME:** Fresnes, Compiègne, Ravensbrück.

Fresnes prison. Would Cicely have realized she was heading north, moving closer toward Alix, closer toward their Paris apartment, but farther than ever from the life she once had? Seven short, insurmountable miles away were the streets and cafés and parks of Paris.

Diana had passed through the corridors of Fresnes at the same time as Cicely. Noor, too, had passed through the cells before them, as did virtually all SOE agents, known or unknown to the others. By then, Geneviève de Gaulle breathed the same stale air at Fresnes prison as Cicely. Betrayed by an agent working with the Gestapo and arrested on Rue Bonaparte in Paris in July 1943, Geneviève was transferred from one prison to another, but not before she was able to dedicate three years to the group *Défense de la France*, help British pilots fallen from the sky find refuge, and write for an illegal newspaper, all the while skirting the city-streets in wartime turmoil. This was her path: Avenue Foch to Fresnes to Compiègne.

Compiègne. A forest lush with beech and oak. It's possible that here, so near Paris, Cicely had ridden horseback in those years before the war. To arrive in Compiègne, a convoy would pass through Paris, but by then any awareness of the proximity of the rue Bosquet could only cause anguish. By the time they arrived at Compiègne, prisoners were able to see faces to go with voices they recognized, for prisoners headed to Compiègne from Fresnes spent the hours before departure in common cells. But for many by that time in the war, the time in Compiègne would not be long. From Compiègne, Diana was delivered to her death at Natzweiler. From Compiègne, Noor traveled to her death at Dachau. From Compiègne, Geneviève and Cicely would be transported to the prison camp they would last inhabit.

February, 1944. A train waits. Down the line, prisoners hear the de Gaulle name called out. They take it as a cry to endure, knowing by that point that any hesitation would ensure instant death. Even so, applause inspired by the presence of Geneviève ripples through an ocean of women. The Germans react with fury, provoking guard dogs to attack. Somewhere in the mêlée, Cicely and Geneviève are hoarded onto the same line of cattle cars.

From the train to Ravensbrück, many captives write letters, or scribble notes, squeezing them through the cracks and holes of the compartments, hoping one of the villagers watching the passage of the human transports with curiosity and suspicion will retrieve their messages and have a good enough heart to send their words of hope or love or despair onward to the name scrawled somewhere on the paper. Cicely either happens to have an ink pen or borrows one that others clamor to use as well. With composure in spite of a year of incarceration and interrogation, and the suspicion of what must be ahead, Cicely hastily scribbles a message crossways on a small sheet of lined ledger paper.

L: This is an amazing detail, Cicely. I have a copy of that note you tossed. In March of 2007, Janine wrote, explaining that this note was delivered to Alix one day in 1944, and that at the time it was the first indication he had of what had become of you, since your letters to him had stopped arriving. Janine still has the original note. This scrap seems to be a popular evidential artifact, for René, Sigrun, and Janine each sent me a copy. I can only imagine how desperate the prisoners on the train must have felt, not knowing what was to come. You must have written the words knowing the possibility of it being confiscated. The message is static and you didn't dare to sign your name. I can tell how shaky your hand was.

> *Dr. Alix Lefort*
> *at 28 Av Bosquet*
> *Paris Fr,*
>> *Left the 20th of Jan for Germany,*
>> *in the convoy of women.*
>> *Good health, good morale.*
>> *Warn the Red Cross to send shoes,*
>> *warm clothes, and food.*

CL: That's right. I tried to put a good spin on the message, fearing repercussions from the guards, were they to discover our indiscretions. Of course, we hadn't actually experienced Ravensbrück yet; we had little idea of what was coming. Good Lord, as history has revealed, the conditions on the "convoy" were anything but healthy, and morale was at an all time low. I also didn't want dear Alix to worry. I can't imagine how the note found its way to the address. Go on with the transport, and tell it like it was.

The season is winter and the unheated train trundles across the frozen landscape. No water, no food, and for a toilet, one oil drum. Eighty women stuffed into each compartment with not enough room to bend a knee, to reach an arm away from their side, to step away from excrement, menstrual flow, urine, vomit, to collapse once death releases them from their torment.

Finally, days later, barriers crash open and fetid air gives way to an arctic blast. Bodies fall to earth, limb upon limb, eyes are blinded by brightness, soft green pine trees lean against a painfully blue sky, and then, as if a joke, there's a brilliant glimpse of lake water, above which rises—for just an instant—the slightest hint of birdsong. Suddenly truncheons crack, dogs snap and snarl, and only faces of death greet the condemned arrivals.

And this: a rising cry of alarm as eyes admit their vision and nostrils receive the scorched odor and minds realize the point of their arrival and ears hear voices wheeze through parched lips: Ravensbrück.

Fifty miles north and somewhat west of Berlin, equidistant between the Baltic Sea and the lake district of Mecklenberg, lies Ravensbrück. In 1934 the Nazi Party purchased land in this picturesque hamlet along the shores of Schwedt Lake. An unhindered view across the lake from Ravensbrück shows the spires and rooftops of the medieval town of Furstenberg, bordered by the Havel River. This area of Ravensbrück is one of the loveliest and most secluded areas in Germany, scattered with lakes, canals and the river. In the early 1930s, it offered attractive surroundings that the SS and their families could enjoy together.

By November 1938, the SS had purchased several hundred acres of land in this area, and a shipment of 500 men and several women arrived from Sachenhausen Concentration Camp to begin construction of Ravensbrück. Six months later, in the spring of the year, the first transport of 867 women arrived from Lichtenberg, and Ravensbrück officially opened as the seventh major concentration camp to begin operation.

By the time Geneviève and Cicely arrive at Ravensbrück, instead of picturesque views of the lake region, prisoners are surrounded by acres of soot and gray barracks crawling with lice and fleas. The population of Ravensbrück has grown from 18,000 to 47,000 within a year. Already paltry conditions have deteriorated to massively appalling. The stench of the living, the dead and the dying, the diseased, decomposed, and burned flesh, fills the air. By the time of liberation, the once pristine blue of Schwedt Lake would be cloudy with ashes from the camp's three crematoria.

Into this world, at the end of the night of February 3rd, 1944, 958 bodies enter, the largest transport of French women to arrive in Ravensbrück. Two among them are Geneviève de Gaulle and Cicely Lefort. The group, known as the Twenty-Seven-Thousands, have prison numbers inked into their luminous wrists, each with the pre-tag of 27. Geneviève, prisoner number 27.372, endures the orientation fewer than 600 steps from Cicely, prisoner number 27.962. Each prisoner is stripped, inspected, shaved, spritzed with frigid water in what is called a shower, issued threadbare clothing—a red political prisoner triangle stitched on a sleeve—and sent to quarantine.

Cicely Lefort rises from sleep to the festive clatter of wooden spoon against iron pot. Anna must be in the kitchen concocting her weekend specialty. Soufflé, this morning, for the aroma of sweet batter rises from below. Already Madame Lefort hears the distant tolling of the lighthouse buoy, and she curls closer to her husband, whose warm breath moistens her sunburned cheek.

No! Coming closer to the surface of awakening, Madame realizes it is not the sound of Anna in the kitchen. How silly, she thinks. Of course, we left St. Cast days ago, where Anna remains. The sounds that awaken Cicely are street noises from below: Paris, never asleep, merely muted for a few hours before sunrise. She does not rest beside her husband. He always arises early in the city. The subtle yellow light playing across her eyelids is not the morning sun breaking over the English Channel, but her husband's reading lamp. Even on the weekend, Alix reviews his patients' charts and applies himself to medical journals.

Too weary to rise to complete awareness, Cicely jostles the blanket that weighs so heavily across her legs. But why such a blanket, when the moisture of air surely leans toward spring? A flicker of movement brings her dangerously close to mindfulness. She resists, but now the weight of the blanket delves into her flesh, and burns like acid. Now, the light teeters toward a shard, and pierces her brain.

The light: a soot-filled cloud; the clang: an empty soup cup; the wooden spoon: a guard's stanchion.

Blanket:body. Thud:bone.

# CAMP

SECRÉTAIRE D'UN MOUVEMENT DE
RÉSISTANCE, MORTE A RAVENSBRUCK
Evelyne ARNEL

MORTE A RAVENSBRUCK
gazée le 2 mars 45
Mme Emilie Tillion

PRISE AU COURS D'UNE MISSION EN
FRANCE, MORTE A RAVENSBRUCK
Cecily Lefort

Andoul drawing of Evelyne, Emilie, and Cicely at Ravensbrück.
*Lefort family collection*

**AN AVERAGE PERSON** on an average day awakens sensibly. One tumbles out of bed easily, while another bolts to the cymbal of an alarm bell; one ascends to a calming melody, leaps toward a baby's plea, greets an unexpected phone call, or answers the urgent need to relieve oneself. Most—at four o'clock in the morning—simply give a squinted glance to the time, rotate to the other shoulder, listen for a moment to the surging aria of birdsong at this universal hour of their awakening, and nestle back into the covers of repose for as long as they can put off the inevitable beginning of another day. Not many give a fleeting thought to where birdsong no longer exists, to mornings of what, for some terrifying years, was a signature of the Holocaust: *l'appel*. Roll call.

The reports are the same, from Dachau to Buchenwald to Auschwitz to Theresienstadt to Ravensbrück. Stories of cold, heat, rain, snow, the starved and the sick and the maimed holding on to that one last thread of survival instinct. Some survive, most don't.

For Cicely and for Geneviève, for Corrie ten Boom, Germaine Tillion, and a baby boy named Billy born in the camp, for Antonina and Anise and Violette and Sunneva, for Hanka and Helena, Urszula, Isa, and for tens of thousands of others at Ravensbrück alone, the roll call arena could have had an imposing view of Schwedt Lake, were it not for the kitchens, the bunker, the crematorium and the gas chamber lined up between the lake and the grounds where women reduced to skeleton forms, jolted from their lice-infested typhus-seeping tiered bunk slats, also line up at 4:00 each morning, terrified or numb—will this be the morning of my death?—and remain standing for hours through all seasons of weather. If they don't die, they eat a light breakfast and go to work. At the end of the day, potato water followed by another *appel*. If they still don't die, they return to the slats and survive the night, until it is time for morning roll call again.

CL: That's right, Lizzie. You're telling it like it was. Now I'm too numb to feel sad.

On a diagram of the layout of Ravensbrück, the women's housing is surrounded by such civil measures as the laundry, the infirmary, kennels, gardens, single-family housing for SS leaders, potato cellars, and an Uckermark youth camp—the concentration camp for girls 16-21, though girls as young as eight were sent there. And then, always, Schwedt Lake, obscured just beyond the concrete barrier. But for the lake, and minus the camp for girls, the same basic plan can be substituted for Noor at Dachau, for Diana at Natzweiler, and for all the wives and sisters and husbands and brothers and sons and daughters and those few remaining grandparents and children at every concentration camp across Europe.

It is during Cicely's entry examination, unscrupulously performed during those shocking introductory arrival hours, that something not right is discovered. Not long after Cicely arrives at Ravensbrück, she is recalled to the infirmary and told that she has stomach cancer. Most likely, the disease has inhabited Cicely's body for years, and is perhaps linked to her inability to have a child. Whatever the case, the consequences from adventure and stress in Cicely's recent years will have masked any symptoms that her body may have exhibited.

Stomach discomfort could be swept aside as nervousness and anxiety for a woman over 40 who trained to be a spy, dropped into a war zone, and navigated enemy territory. So, too, nausea can be assigned to nervous tension. By the time cancer consumes Cicely, her imprisonment, beatings, and interrogations will be reason enough for bloating or vomiting. Weight loss, too, would not seem unusual.

By early 1944, when Cicely enters Ravensbrück, already perverse medical experiments have taken place at the camp's infirmary. Since 1942, rumor passed through the barracks about *les petite lapins*, little rabbits, young polish girls whose legs are broken and ravaged in order to place gangrené bacteria in the open abrasion to simulate battlefield wounds, so that the effect of treatment could be documented.

Knowledge of experimental operations flourish, carried out by Dr. Stumpfegger who, using surgical equipment such as a hammer to break bones, sever muscles, and amputate limbs, thus crippling the subject in order to study potential transplants and prosthetic attachments for German soldiers. Other staff, perhaps bored, experiment with prisoners for such ploys as a remedy for acute hypothermia. These cases involve placing half-frozen naked male prisoners between naked female prisoners and forcing sexual stimulation so the possibility for resuscitation can be judged.

Cicely's condition comes to the notice of one of the camp's senior medical doctors, Percival Treite. Because Cicely does not exactly fit into the typical criteria attached to this form of cancer—as a Caucasian female under the age of 45—the SS doctor might suspect a form of H. pylori bacteria or the influence of pernicious anemia due to a lack of B12. These statistics could appeal to his professional curiosity as a man of medicine.

It is possible that Cicely actually receives more humane treatment as an experimental patient than she was subjected to as just another number in the overcrowded camp barracks. Indeed, Cicely survives the surgery, receives a thicker porridge than previously, and for a brief reprieve, sleeps in the relatively sanitary conditions of the infirmary as opposed to the squalor of barracks.

The end of the year 1944. Although unknown to the prisoners in work camps and death camps across the continent, Allied forces have begun liberating parts of Western Europe. German leadership has to deal with the problem of human baggage in the territories being lost, and the process of dissolution speeds up. Tension and nervousness break down the focus of medical experimentation, and Cicely is returned to Block 13.

1944 blends into 1945. January becomes February. One day is like another. Survival is recorded only by hours of dark and darker, cold and colder, sick and sicker. Camp conditions worsen, treatment becomes even more brutal—there can hardly be any fewer rations— and bodies are packed off to the gas chamber and crematorium at an ever increasing rate. At Ravensbrück, pink slips are being delivered. Dr. Treite sees Cicely's name on the list. Those who receive such a notice are sent to the Jugendlager, health camps designated for convalescence. But no such destinations exist. The pink slip is a direct ticket to the gas chamber.

The doctor, however, does not want the successful results of his experimental study to disappear. He requisitions a nurse, Mary Lindell de Monchy, a prisoner and former escape-line organizer who knows Cicely, to transfer her to another group in camp, but, like Cammaerts's request in 1943 for Cicely's return to England, the recall is received too late. Though the form arrives for Cicely and two of her friends to be brought back to the main camp, one of the friends, Mary Young, has given up. Cicely, attending to her with the hope of convincing her friend to leave also, is left behind. Only Mary O'Shaugnessy is returned to the main camp, and she survived the war.

CL: And Ms. Young and I did not. We were certainly not alone in that regard.

L: I know. I know. Transport trucks pulled up outside the infirmary. Patients, such as you and Mary, too weak to struggle or care any longer, were loaded onto the lorries heading to the furnace. In other parts of camp, as word spread of the selection taking place, some of the women took a white sleeping powder. Growing heaps of gray bodies piled up.

Cicely, you will soon join the dead. You will not even be so much as a number counted. Your end bears no witness. White powder? Loss of a will to live? The gas chamber? Some accounts mark your death as January, others as February. This much is known of your passing:

You are simply gone, as if it were that easy.

CL: Please, don't leave it like this. Tell me another story. Sing me a song. Write me a dream.

L: Shhhh. Cicely, listen! Through the open window: birdsong. Do you hear?

If Alix could have willed a peaceful death for his wife, as the moment of blackness enveloped her, it might be this:

A rising and consuming brightness. Her mother, Margaret, waves to Cicely from the veranda of their home in Bayswater. Beneath Margaret's ringlets of hair flickers a pale mauve ribbon. Winston, the blackest of the Chows, leaps toward Cicely and barks, willing her to play. Afternoon luster shimmers off the high banks of windows in streaks of gold. A Common Whitethroat warbles from a Chestnut tree. Cicely, the child, does not know that this is the last day she will live in England, for the next morning Margaret will leave their home and take her daughter to France. This last day, when Cicely flourishes in the innocence of childhood, she remembers something so simple and childlike as rolling down the gently terraced garden while her bearish dog weaves his way around her, like the fingers of ribbon that twine their way through her mother's hair.

Night becomes day.

And songbirds return to Paris.

# PART TWO

# THE ENGLISH FILES

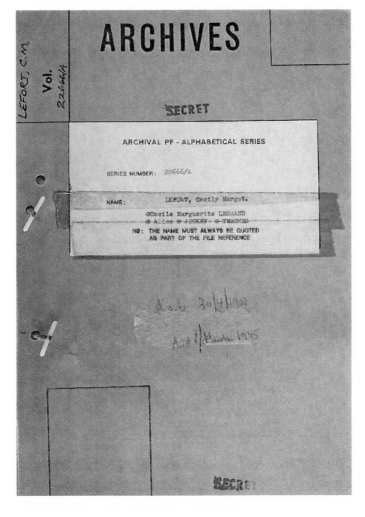

SOE Archive cover.
*Dr. David Murphy*

# I. DEEPER REVELATIONS

Author peering into the Leforts' former office
and home at Avenue Bosquet.
*Elizabeth Sloan*

**CL: THAT WAS HARD.**

L: I'm glad that part's over with.

CL: And now? The truth?

L: The truth is something we can never know. The truth is, I may have to put my loyalty to you on reserve, to make way for new-found loyalties.

CL: Alix's new family?

L: The truth is this: that what we have may be as close to the truth as we can get. My archives will help.

February, 2009.
Cicely's SOE documents finally arrive in my mailbox from Dr. Murphy in Ireland. I've had these files for four days now, and am having trouble wrapping my head around the possibilities for reinterpretation. I am at first elated to have more of the inside story, but as each day passes—each day in which every available hour is occupied with delving through the letters, trying to translate enough to supply some understanding until I can meet with a translator in a couple weeks—I fall deeper into despair over how to reconcile the intensifying conflicts.

With this fresh arrival of more "evidence" about Cicely's life during WWII, reconsideration is necessary. Reflection is unavoidable. Perspective is crucial.

I recall a subtle and brief mention in one of Jimmy Close's early letters that perhaps all was not well between Cicely and Alix and their marriage. Where would he have gotten this notion? I dismissed it, due to lack of evidence, and because I didn't want to go down that path. Cicely died. What good would recognizing a flaw in her marriage serve?

> For now we see through a glass, darkly;
> but then face to face: now I know in part;
> but then shall I know even as also I am known.
> *Corinthians 13 King James Version*

The recovered correspondence reveals both answers and questions. These 136 documents become part of Cicely's story as testament to the tragedy of war on all fronts, including the death of affection, the end of some relationships, the beginning of others. And so once again, I continue the thread that leads me toward understanding the life, and death (murder), of Cicely Margot Gordon Lefort.

Life can be complicated even on the most simple of days. Add love and commitment, add the drama of war and the passion it can ignite, add a world of dreams and hopes, disappointment and fear, add what appears to be the truth, and then come out on the other side exhausted and defeated, but also relieved and joyful. Then try to explain these emotions, to yourself, to others. Feel the pull of conflict. Try not to turn away.

This is how it works. Documents arrive, to be sorted, organized, collated, chipped away at for some semblance of translation, only for the witness to reorganize, reinterpret, recollate, wait. I wait now for part of this collection, the French letters from Alix in his attempt after the war to track Cicely's path, to be translated.

Say you believe you understand, but soon realize that this territory is something that no one will truly understand; not even, you believe, those closest to the drama, the original characters who played out this journey. What has been denied is this collective and historical perspective that I now possess.

CL: One would think, what with Mother's flamboyant life, and my own questionable paternity, that I would be prepared for possible upcoming revelations. But of course, "face to face" brings everything closer to home, closer to the heart, closer to the bone. Tread gently, but proceed.

L: That day many years ago already, when one of Janine and Alix's daughters sent me photographs of both you and Alix, each in your war uniforms, I cut and pasted your images side by side on one piece of paper. I thought I had achieved the one thing most in the world that you ever wanted: to be together again.

I am beginning to learn otherwise. Though this saddens me, I am also reconciled with it because I have learned how the story ends, or more appropriately, how the story continued. I learned it from the very woman who, along with Alix, honored your life for all these decades since your death.

And then there's what Sigrún believes, or anyway, what she feels. No, dear, I have not forgotten about your Iceland confidante.

CL: I was wondering when you'd get back to her. Please, don't misinterpret my feelings. I am indebted to Sigrún Lilja. It's just that, she does know things, things I wasn't sure I ever wanted to talk about. I've denied that part of my life for so long, I'm not so sure that I even remember it clearly. "Through a glass, darkly...."

L: Sigrún suggested that all was not as congenial with your marriage as I had wanted to believe. Jimmy Close made the same indication. As we're yet to see, your cousin Kitty confirms the intention. I fought it, but have come to realize that it's best to accept in order to understand the full meaning of your life.

Because I now hold copies of the actual Red Cross papers, I can see the series of stamps and postal cancellations and dates, the journey these war missives took. The message goes out from you and eventually, oftentimes in a matter of months, returns with Alix's response typed on the back of the original.

I am noticing, only now, that all these messages were originally sent from you, to Alix, and he does not appear to initiate the communication. Perhaps that was just the way of Red Cross during the war, accessible to you more easily than to Alix. (But how did he return the document to you, with his message typed on the back? Through Red Cross in Paris?) Nevertheless, each original overleaf is typed on official Red Cross letterhead. Note that each of these categories is printed in English, French, and German. Cicely, your message is typed to Alix in French, but for translation purposes, English will suffice. Also note, even in this one message, coming from you, that your name is spelled two ways:

*War Organisation of the British Red Cross and Order of St. John*
*Sender: Cecily Lefort, from Clarence House, St. James London*

*Message (not more than 25 words)*

*Date Jan 11, 1943*
> *Impossible to write*
> *Sending good health*
> *I am very well*
> *Received your news of November 2*
> *I see Aline tomorrow*
*Affectionate thoughts for you*
*Cecile*

L: This message did not arrive in Paris until March 12, and was returned to you with a message from Alix dated April 19, typed on the back side, but you would not receive this for another four months after he wrote:

*April 19, 1943*
> *The morale situation very bad because correspondence*
> *impossible*
> *I am well but this prolonged absence is a catastrophe*
> *for the two of us*
*Affectionate thoughts*
*Lefort*

C.L: No more "I kiss you with all my heart," or even the familiar "Alix," but a detached "Lefort" signature. I see.

L: Cicely, love. I know that when all the world was in a swirl around you, and recruitment was random and sporadic, that neither you, nor Alix, would ever have fathomed how all this news and these messages and the files I now possess might one day come to light, with such disparate parts coming together, to reveal such a conflicting story.

So here's what I have in relation to these most recent messages between you and Alix. Yes, you wrote the rather detached message on January 11, but what I also have here in this stack of Red Cross papers, is an application for employment, filled out by you, requesting to be an "agent in the Field after training." This application is dated January 8, three days before you sent that noncommittal message to your husband.

CL: But dear, it's all I could do! I did not know if I would be accepted, and as you well know by now, indeed if I was accepted, I could not divulge this information to Alix, or anyone. Yes, the ways of war are limited and strange.

L: I'm going to sound like "the devil's advocate," I know, and truly I do not mean to be. I'm just so curious about how all these pieces fall into place. Please believe me, Cicely, that I intend no harm to your feelings. You are my lovely family, more so now than ever. It seems that the threads just kept unraveling, out of anyone's control. In truth, this is what intrigues me.

You are a mysterious woman. (I adore that about you, Cicely!) On this document, you use Kitty's address at Square Acres as your permanent residence, which was certainly true for war time; for previous employment, you wrote "receptionist to surgeon in Paris," but apparently did not indicate that the surgeon was your husband? Although the form does list a husband being French, but under "particulars of relatives now living in enemy-occupied or controlled countries," the space is left blank, and again there is no reference to Alix.

But we have this whole stack of documents, so let's see what else we discover.

CL: Carry on, Lizzie. As you point out, I was not even aware of this jumble of information that was building and becoming a record of my life. You now have me pulled into the web just as much as you are.

L: This next paper might not please you much. It includes various trainers' interpretations of your "performance," and is not entirely favorable:

*February 15, 1943 Agent Reviews:*

Lt. Tongue: "This student looks vague; mixed quite well; is interested in the course and could be relied on to be loyal but doubt if she has enough initiative to achieve much. Spinsterish but kind. Would like to remain a F.A.N.Y. and is suitable."

D/CE.3 to MT.2 (And you, Cicely, were anonymously identified as 27 X.15; already the need to code and decode was in order.): "There is no security objection for this student proceeding to Group B. Please inform Group B that X.15 has been reported to be rather a chatterbox but discreet about her work."

Lt. Tongue: "Has a number of friends in common with X.4 in 27 land. Talkative?"

L: I'm sorry, Cicely, but "in 27 land"? This sounds like The Wizard of Oz: "We're not in Kansas anymore."

CL: You must trust, dear cousin, that there was always a reason to the rhyme of codes. SOE's code for France was 27. I trained as a member of Party 27X. The answer to the riddle of course is that 27 land meant in France! Ah, I must admit I do miss those conundrums and evasive actions.

Speaking of riddles. The wizard of what? Kansas? (Yes, of course I do know Kansas is a state in the United States of America, dear, but why are *we* not there anymore?)

L: Right, I keep forgetting....

L/Cpl Gordon, Group B (Just a common enough surname I suppose, not to be confused with you; though of course, there was no reference to your family name of Gordon on any papers, was there, just that slip of MacKenzie a while back?): "Very ladylike, very English in spite of French background, has a wide circle of friends amongst quite well known and influential people, politicians, gens du monde, artists of the Salon School, all very respectable. Inclined to blurt out things in a rather embarrassing way, which she probably would not have said if she had thought first."

CL: Madame Lizzie. What can I say? Yes, I did hold on to my British ways (*c'est la vie!*), yes, my connections did include influential politicians and artists, and yes, I did like to chat. (At times, this "character flaw" aggravated Alix to no end.) However, if I appeared spinsterish, that was afterall an SOE ruse. Plain was the name of Vera's game for agents dropping into enemy territory, so looking like a...what was it Bunny had said? A pastor's wife for heaven sake? Well, that worked in my favor. (Oh please, do forgive my feathers getting ruffled. I could be attractive when I cleaned myself up. How could I not have had some level of good looks, what with the beauty my mother was, and Granny being so handsome. And a certain Dr. Lefort found me irresistible, for a time being, anyway.) Nevertheless, as history has recorded, I passed the qualifications, didn't I!

L: No worry about your ruffled feathers, my dear. Honestly, it does us both good to see that you still have some gumption. But back to these SOE records.

Another month goes by, you've been in training, building up to whatever mission you would be assigned. You write another message to Alix. By then of course you are fully ensconced at Wanborough House, leading a very secret life. Here is the next document, written March 12, 1943, from England, but not received in France until nearly a month later, on April 9, 1943:

> *Happy to receive news that you are well*
> *Will see Aline Fox*
> *Give my greeting to Anna*
> *Affectionate thoughts*
> *Cecile*

L: A few weeks later, on May 24, 1943, Alix returned a note to you on the back, and you might have received it around June 25,

1943, but that was almost a week after you had left England for good, and entered France into enemy territory:

> *I despair*
> *This long abandonment has broken everything*
> *I do not think a return is possible*
> *I will explain everything soon*
> *Friendly thoughts*
> *Lefort*

CL: And I never did receive his explanation, at no fault to either of us, perhaps just the fault of war.

L: There's more. I have your "application for promotion," dated May 6, for training to be an "agent in the field." On May 19th—you must have been excited, and perhaps quite nervous considering the possible repercussions—when you received this formal acceptance, printed on Air Ministry, London, W.C.2. crested letterhead:

*Madam,*

> *I am commanded by the Air Council to inform you that they have approved your appointment to an Honorary Commission in the Women's Auxiliary Air Force in the rank of Assistant Section Officer. The appointment . . . will be effective from the 14th of May, 1943.*

L: This document goes on to say there will be no pay, no allowances, and no benefits, and that you will be enrolled on a civilian basis.

After this, there seems to be a gap in documents included in your SOE file, because the next form in this deep stack of your papers is dated August 20, 1943. (Yes, this is two months already past your time in the field as an agent, and only one month before your unfortunate capture.) See how quickly—I am rather alarmed how quickly—you went from civilian with no pay, to secret agent in the Field and entered in the salary books! At the top, in red capital letters, and underlined, it reads:

*PRIVATE & CONFIDENTIAL* (followed by a heavy black lined box stamped):
*ENTERED IN SALARIES BOOK.*
*Salary Agent Abroad – Mrs. C. M. Lefort*
This agent left for the Field on 16.6.43.

While in the Field, her rate of sterling pay is £300 per annum to be banked quarterly in advance. Will you, therefore, please bank as soon as possible the sum as per statement attached, covering pay for the period 17.6/30.9.43, and on 1.10.43 and quarterly thereafter until further notice, the sum of £75?

Her account is with:
Lloyd's Bank Ltd.,
16 St. James, W.1.

CL: Yes, the war effort was picking up speed, practically by the hour, especially with Operation Overlord being planned. I see now, watching you shuffle through this file you have so diligently collected, how the momentum begins to take on a life of its own, with my life soon to be very much not of my own. I continue to be fascinated by my own journey.

L: There are still a few Red Cross messages, here toward the end of the stack that you sent before you left for the fields of France, but these were also not returned from Alix until it was too late for you to read. This jumbled mix of messages crossing the waters between England and France, missing connection to both you and Alix, provides quite the web of intrigue and *what ifs*. And now, finally, here in this light of day so many decades later, you can see how the pieces fit for the first time.

CL: May I view the next document please? I see now how you are able to track the dates of messages sent and received by comparing dates typed in black on the records and stamped in red ink on the overleaf forms. So I sent this message on May 13, 1943, and I see here that it arrived in France on June 1, 1943. That's less than two weeks. A much quicker delivery than most of the others. Perhaps the frequency of air drops was picking up with the quicker pace of war activities, dropping off messages and agents at the same time. I wonder why I apologize for the mail delays. I see here that I wrote:

> *I regret that you do not receive any news*
> *I am very well*
> *I live at the moment with Win Feely*
> *I often see Aline*
> *Affectionate thoughts to you*
> *Cecile Lefort*

L: Go easy on yourself, Cicely. I read your regret, not as an apology, for you hold no fault, but as a sadness of the reality that the war is what it is, making communication unbearably difficult. But I do wonder why you signed so formally, and also why you wrote "affectionate thoughts to you" and not just "affectionate thoughts," as you did in all your other messages. You must have realized that your days in England were numbered, knowing that the call to drop into France could come at any time, and you meant to be specific. And still, you could say none of this to your husband. The mention that you were living with Win Feely must have been a "veil" as well, to hide the activities you were involved with. (Who is this Win Feely, and who is Aline that you often mention?)

CL: I must admit that at this far removed distance, Win and Aline seem foggy and insignificant, considering all that has happened since. I'm more interested in connecting my SOE assignments with these dates. I see it was on June 22 that Alix returned his reply. That would be when I was five days back in France, having already moved quickly in and out of Paris, not a moment available to find Alix. Would that the opportunity had presented itself, perhaps all this mystery and misunderstanding could have been cleared up, one way or another, for a different outcome in our relationship. But that was not to be.

Please, Lizzie, you must read this one for me. Just a glimpse, and I'm certain the message is grim.

L: Let me take a look. Oh yes, this is a tough one for you to read. Here is what Alix wrote that day:

> *I think that you cannot come back*
> *This long absence must create other affections*
> *I am very pained What is there to do?*

Lefort

CL: The direction his life was going is beginning to be revealed. What turmoil he was in, not knowing what to say, how to disclose the turn of events, how much he should protect my feelings, how much to let go. And never a word from me in reply to what he was trying to say. Alix must have felt quite dismissed, indeed. *Oy vey.*

L: Yes, but Alix continued to wait, believing that at some point the news of his feelings had arrived in your hands.

CL: I can't seem to stop wondering, even after all this time, what must have been going through my husband's mind. What *could* he have been thinking? Oh gosh, all this wondering, as if we ever can know what truly goes on inside anyone's head. But you, my dear Lizzie, seem to have an art for digging deeper than anyone I've ever known.

What? Ah, right. To clarify, for anyone I've ever known who wasn't a professional mind tapper, as in a secret agent, or a spy trainer!

L: Thank you (I think). Here's my go at what Alix *must* have been thinking: Surely Cicely will respond soon? Whatever can she be thinking? How will she interpret "other affections"? Is she ignoring my frustration and confusion? Does she not care about my feelings? Does she understand how this separation and the drama of living in an occupied city require compassion and camaraderie, of which I have lacked since she left France in June of 1940? Does she not recognize, consider, or wish to address these issues?

CL: So we're all just speculating about what everyone else is thinking. Almost a comedy, but for the outcomes, don't you think?

But you may be right. I remember now his words, after his dear mother died: "I would need so much to have you close to me," but I was not there for him then, either. Perhaps I'm getting sentimental in my old age.

Here's another clue I'm noticing, Lizzie. In this, and in some of his later messages, Alix uses the French *il* when he writes to me, as if he's referring to himself in third person. He is emotionally removing himself from my life, step by step.

L: So much life was being lived, separately, and often tentatively, by both you and Alix. Neither of you could know or even remember which message was sent when and what was conveyed, only to have your intentions overlap and repeat and become lost between the two of you.

And then, this document, sent to you as Mrs. C. Lefort on Wimpole Street in London. This, my dear, dear Cicely, may be the toughest to read so far:

*August 7th, 1943*
*Dear Madam,*

> *We are writing to inform you that we have just received the following communication from the International Red Cross at Geneva:*

> *We would be thankful for you to get in touch with Mme Lefort, at the home of Mrs. R.A. Graham, Square Acres, on behalf of Dr. Lefort, 28, Avenue Bosquet in Paris:*

> *The situation of the abandonment of his home has put him in a situation he can't stand anymore. The communal life before was a terrible deception — His hope now is to be able to remake a home with the goal of having children.*

> *He is counting on her understanding, affection and loyalty for him, and she will quickly write a letter, giving him explicit consent that will allow him to proceed with a divorce and an annulment.*

> *This letter could only serve to make formalities to hasten, and he prays that she will excuse this brutal letter*

*but these are exceptional circumstances. He hopes with all his heart that Cecile will hold him and his affections in high esteem.*

*We enclose also a reply to a postal message sent by you on 12.3.43. If you wish to send Dr. Lefort a longer message than the usual 25 words, we shall be glad to send it by special letter to the International Red Cross. We could in this way send about forty to fifty words. We could also arrange to transmit any documents which you may wish to have sent to him.*

*Awaiting your reply, and assuring you of our readiness to help you in any way we can,*
*Yours faithfully,*
*Muriel Monkhouse*
*French Section*

CL: Oh my. Alix always had a way with words. "Brutal" indeed! Remind me, Lizzie, he did not understand that I was not ignoring his messages leading up to this request, but I (simply) did not receive them. Ah, yes, but what was I doing? Indeed, I was not behaving like a good wife. I was going off to be a spy for heaven's sake! What was I thinking? Ah, but Alix didn't know that I had done that yet! Oh my, oh my. Such dire paths arise from the arbitrary paths we take.

L: I know. I know. Even if you had remained in England, the receipt of this news would have been quite upsetting to you. I find it curious also that apparently the French Section and SOE headquarters did not share agendas, for Muriel Monkhouse obviously also had no idea that you, the recipient of this news and Alix's wife, were no longer in London, or even on British soil. The French Section seems to assume though that you, having received this petition, would summarily acquiesce with no further ado, and transmit divorce papers forthwith. Ms. Monkhouse's "kind" offer to allow up to fifty words instead of the standard 25 seems dismissive of the world of emotions she surely would realize this decree might procure.

I see my loyalties to you are returning with complete bias at the moment. This letter certainly does set a whole new facet of complications into motion. Follow along, Cicely. In spite of any hurt, we may find a bit of dark humor on this journey, only because of the advantage of our historical position for this overview.

The following day, August 8, SOE in London was dealing with the ripples Muriel's forwarding of the message from France was creating. The request for divorce had to be read and had to be dealt with by your commanding officer, since you were nowhere to be found. The coded names keep the identities obscure—for example the undisclosed F.L. is responsible for many of these messages—but perhaps some individuals will fall into place as the documents pile up. This one was sent to D/CE.2, from F.L. At the top of the paper is the clandestine category, Most Secret.

# II. MOST SECRET

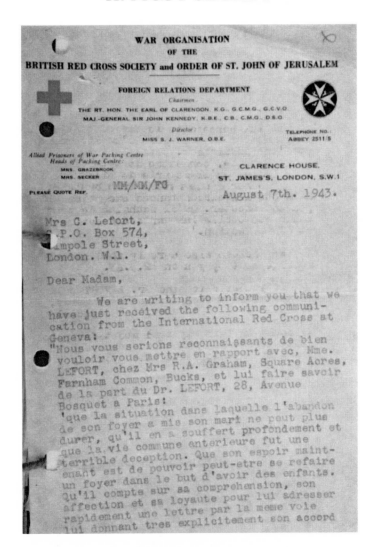

WAR ORGANISATION
OF THE
BRITISH RED CROSS SOCIETY and ORDER OF ST. JOHN OF JERUSALEM

FOREIGN RELATIONS DEPARTMENT
*Chairmen*
THE RT. HON. THE EARL OF CLARENDON. K.G., G.C.M.G., G.C.V.O.
MAJ.-GENERAL SIR JOHN KENNEDY, K.B.E., C.B., C.M.G., D.S.O.

*Director*
MISS S. J. WARNER, O.B.E.

TELEPHONE NO.:
ABBEY 2511/5

*Allied Prisoners of War Packing Centre*
*Heads of Packing Centre:*
MRS. GRAZEBROOK
MRS. SECKER

CLARENCE HOUSE,
ST. JAMES'S, LONDON, S.W.1

PLEASE QUOTE REF.    MM/MM/FG

August 7th. 1943.

Mrs C. Lefort,
P.O. Box 574,
Wimpole Street,
London. W.1.

Dear Madam,

We are writing to inform you that we
have just received the following communication from the International Red Cross at
Geneva:

"Nous vous serions reconnaissants de bien
vouloir vous mettre en rapport avec, Mme.
LEFORT, chez Mrs R.A. Graham, Square Acres,
Farnham Common, Bucks, et lui faire savoir
de la part du Dr. LEFORT, 28, Avenue
Bosquet a Paris:

'que la situation dans laquelle l'abandon
de son foyer a mis son mari ne peut plus
durer, qu'il en a souffert profondement et
que la vie commune anterieure fut une
terrible deception. Que son espoir maint-
enant est de pouvoir peut-etre se refaire
un foyer dans le but d'avoir des enfants.
Qu'il compte sur sa comprehension, son
affection et sa loyaute pour lui adresser
rapidement une lettre par la meme voie
lui donnant tres explicitement son accord

SOE file, War Office petition for divorce.
*Dr. David Murphy*

**L: HERE IS THAT "MOST SECRET" MESSAGE** sent to D/CE.2 from F.L.:

> Enclosed is the letter from the Red Cross about which I spoke to you. I feel it is evading the issue merely to ignore this, particularly as Dr. Lefort must know quite well that his messages have not failed to reach Mrs. Lefort in the past (see attached messages). Mrs. Lefort is now working for us in the south of France. Before she left she asked us to send Red-Cross messages to her husband about once a month. In view of Dr. Lefort's letter it is obviously impossible for us to do this. I should be most grateful for any suggestion you can make.

L: On August 17, nine days later, F.L. replies to D/CE.2 with this curt response:

> I return herewith your papers. I am strongly of the opinion that the communication should be completely ignored.

Is it out of line for me, Cicely, to think, "Poor Alix?"

I know, I know, the sadness the situation produces for all parties, but when I can remove myself and be an objective moderator, I also have empathy for your husband. The headquarters can't inform Alix of your work as an agent, for it would put everyone involved in SOE and other resistance circuits at serious risk, and the consequences were too noteworthy to consider.

CL: And that's it, isn't it?

L: As far as recorded correspondence between you and Alix, I believe so. Alix was left with no reply (from you) to his request, which might have aggravated him to no end, but even if you had been able to send a communication, what could you say? Your journey into darkness is closing in as well.

CL: Yes, this is the point where Gestapo finds me, I travel through the prison and interrogation systems, and finally....

L: The impending finality of your situation is clear. But you are being tracked by SOE and at some point of course, Alix has been alerted to the situation. Let's follow that path and see how it played out. The next report in your file, and this is as original and official as it gets, is dated November 11, 1943, from Roger (Francis Cammaerts), received by bag from Berne. This is Roger's regular report, so not all is about you, Cicely, but you get "#1 billing," and historically, what was going on all around is intriguing. Here is the SOE report of circumstances at the time of your arrest:

> *Fifth report September 20, 1943*
>     1. <u>Arrest of ALICE</u>. ALICE was arrested Wednesday 15, 1943, at the house of DAUJAT at MONTÉLIMAR. Contrary to advice she arrived there at 4.00 a.m. instead of going to his office during the day. He managed to save all compromising material, but she had in her bag a paper, the contents of which I am ignorant, but which certainly did not contain any addresses as she was always very careful in this matter. She could not explain this paper and was taken for questioning. DAUJAT himself escaped by window at rear and nothing compromising fell into hands of Gestapo. This arrest may be consequence of arrest of _____courier, or of denunciation by personal enemy known to have been intimate with Gestapo recently. This man has been dealt with. Have warned all who were in contact with ALICE and all precautions have been taken. Am taking all measures possible to keep trace of ALICE but have no means of direct information. If you have anyone capable of inside work with Gestapo will you attend to this. Meanwhile, I can only say she was arrested by detachments whose H.Q. is at ST. ETIENNE. I deeply regret this event as ALICE had worked very

well. In my defence I can only say that security measures I advised were not followed. Unless she had some direct evidence on her of which I am ignorant, they have no means of knowing who she was except her papers.

2. <u>Operations this moon</u>. Message for ROCHEMAURE ground passed night of 18.[th] A plane passed at 0010 hrs but as we were late due to disorganization caused by arrest of ALICE lamps were not properly in line; in spite of my signal plane passed on; nothing else heard till 4:00. Next night I was not there but apparently operation at ROCHEMAURE and CLEAN D'ANDRAN passed off alright. Message for BORDAUX passed but you said nothing of this in your telegram. Can acknowledge receipt of seven containers and one package COUSEGAULES, but why only seven when fifteen were ordered? BEAUREPAIRE had instructions to receive as last month. Will send news of this failure as soon as I am informed.

3. <u>Project mentioned at VALENSOL</u>. Have very reliable staff of officers for this work, including aviation expert who assures me that on this plain at least one thousand gliders per hour or two hundred transport planes could be received. If ground is ploughed or obstructed, have full means of dealing with this at short notice large tractors available. Can man this scheme at will as I have a very large selection of guerrillas on whom I can draw; will adapt plan to suit operation proposed. Route from VALENSOL to AVIGNON can be protected if attack proposed in that direction. Please inform at earliest and prepare operations for arms and provisions for men needed in this region. A German H.Q. is nearby on the plain; all necessary measures can be taken to wipe them out.

4. <u>Prepare operation</u>. COUSEGAULES ground October 30 containers.

    5.  <u>Personnel</u>.  Please  send  instructions  re
CLAUDEL and ALAIN by telegram at earliest.

    6.  <u>Old Organisation</u>. Have sound information
that very dangerous man is in intimate contact with
_____ who was PAUL'S lieutenant and is now
working in North. Believe that _____ has
asked to have GERVAIS work with him. Advise you
send no one to this circuit without circumspection.
Man concerned called CHAILLANT has been arrested
and escaped. Was in close touch with German officer
who arranged arrest of RAOUL and LISE. He still
claims that this officer is sincere and story of his
escape is very doubtful.

    7.  Will continue work of R.A.F. on viaduct at
ANTHEOR unless ordered to contrary. Trains are
running normally now. Can instruct expert engineer
who disposes of material sufficient to handle this.

CL: Oh my! Only moments ago, Lizzie, I asked you, "WHAT
WAS I DOING?"

Well here is your answer: This! THIS is what I was doing. I was
living a life of adventure and purpose. Do you see the energy and
camaraderie, the sense of duty to defend all that we loved, by being
involved with the war effort, and in the immediate action? Yes, dear
Lizzie. Thank you. Thank you. Roger's report here just reminded me
of why I was willing to risk all, even at the expense of my marriage,
indeed my life.

L: A life well lived, love. Sitting at my desk typing Roger's report
made my heart beat rapidly, as if the moment was upon me. Just
copying his words letter by letter brought to life the tap tap tap at his
typewriter, any misplaced punctuation (of which there were very
few, and I am impressed) was part of the forward movement, his
focus on reporting all details and conveying correct codes.

CL: You told me that Raymond Daujat died after train sabotage.
It might have been a mission that followed up from this report, don't
you think?

L: Indeed. And still to come, Alix's desperate search to find out what happened to you, in fact for him to understand how you ever came to such a situation. One can only imagine how surreal his entire ordeal had become. I will continue through your English file, and track the course of events. This is what was going on all around you, surrounding the awful path your life was taking. Imagine this in real time, when no one yet knew the outcome, and how the pieces continue to build upon each other to reveal a narrative. At this point, there is a gap of nearly a year gap in these documents.

Here then is the first official record on file of your capture, following Roger's report back in September 1943. This paper is dated July 25, 1944:

SOE BATTLE CASUALTY

*name* C.M. Lefort
*casualty date* 15.9.43
*aliases* Cecile Marguerite Legrand. (Teacher)
*birth* British, 30.4.1900. London
*section* F
*service* A/S.O., W.A.A.F.
*nature of casualty* Arrested
*nature and place of operation* Courier. Montélimar
*last known to be free* 14.9.43
*source of report* Her organizer in the Field. Reliable
*last known addresses* Docteur Alix Lefort, (Husband). Mrs. R.A. Graham, (Aunt)
*remarks* In prison, Toulouse. (5.11.43 from Field). Later report (19.4.44) states may have been sent to Germany.

CL: So there it is, the end of the journey I took. Continue, please, with what else you came to realize from the perspective of my loved ones.

L: There was a lot of activity, mostly activated from your cousin, Kitty (Mrs. R.A. Graham, identified as Aunt in report above) on your behalf. This post is dated August 12, 1944, from Square Acres, with the flawed allusion of your good health:

*Dear Sirs.*
        *I have received a Red X message from Dr. Alix Lefort
in Paris, saying that his wife, Mrs. Cicely M. Lefort, is
now a prisoner in Germany. Address given is Frauen-
Konzentration-Lager No. 27962 Bloc 13 Ravensbrück bei
Furstenberg Mecklenburg. Deutschland. The message says
"Cicely en bonne santé." I am sending this information in
case it is of interest to you and for the future arrangement
of Dr. Lefort's correspondence. I am her cousin, and of
British Nationality by birth.*
*Yours truly,*
*M. M. B. Graham. (Mrs. R.A. Graham.)*

L: August 17, Major I.K. Mackenzie, Wimpole Street, London,
sends this message to Mrs. R.A. Graham:

*Dear Madam,*
        *Thank you for your letter of August 12, giving us
news of Mrs. Cicely M. Lefort received through Dr. Alix
Lefort in Paris.*
        *I think it may be advisable not to write to her from
here, especially at this stage of the war. We are very happy
to know that she is well and shall be grateful if you will
forward any further information you may receive on her.
In her best interests, please do not initiate any enquiries
thorough the Red X. and refer all matters to me.*
*With renewed thanks. Yours truly,*
*Maj. Mackenzie*

L: August 22, this reply from Kitty, still known to Major Mackenzie
as Mrs. R. A. Graham:

        *Dear Sir. Thank you for your letter of August 17. I
have not made any enquiries through the Red X. about
Mrs. C.M.Lefort but have been considering sending a
message through their service. Presumably she counts as
French...but the Germans know she's Dr. Lefort's English*

*wife and that he has sent me a Red X. message giving me her address. M. Lefort has been completely discreet but I have 3 daughters, two of whom were + one still is living in the country (so to speak!) + I realize the need for caution. Unless you say its all right I will not try to send the Red X. messages + will certainly send you any further information, but suppose it will only come when Dr. Lefort can write direct from Paris or his wife is free to do so. I will warn others not to write to her.*

*Yrs. Truly,*
*M. M. B. Graham*

L: August 26, the correspondence continues with this in-house memo, to F/INT from D/CE.G.1:

*I return Mrs. Graham's letter. There is no objection to replying to a Red Cross message as long as great care is taken that the reply adds no information which the Censorship cannot have derived already from the message being answered. For example, there can be no objection to referring to any one mentioned in the original letter, but no additional people had better be mentioned in the reply. It is difficult in fact to see that a normally discreet reply can do any harm and we are possibly being over cautious in these cases, but I am sure that this is the right policy — if anything goes wrong we must be sure that it is not the result of anything we have done.*

L: And then, Cicely, no papers until the end of November. (At some point, Cicely, I would like to correlate just where you were at the times of these letters, but that can wait.) I know you will have comments, but for now, let's keep the rhythm going.

Next is a handwritten letter from Kitty, in reply to Major MacKenzie. It looks like someone has written at the top of this letter a reference to correspondence of August 17 and October 12. Perhaps that October 12 letter will still show up. Also note, these letters are written in fountain pen script, so even English translation can be difficult.

*Nov 30th 1944*

 *Dear Major MacKenzie. You asked me to let you have any further news I might receive about Mrs. Cicely Lefort— probably you have all the information that you require, but this morning I had the first letter from her husband, Dr. Alix Lefort, in Paris. He says:*

 *You certainly know the terrible catastrophe that has happened to Cicely. I was informed of this horrible news about a year ago when she had arrived in Montilemar. Could you, by an intermediary, address some packages to her? I wasn't able since I don't know her address. During these four months I have no other means to relieve my pain. She reclaimed the packages that had food and warm clothing. We have to write to Germany. God she must get out of this horrible camp. How is it that she got into this terrible situation? What was her idea to return to France? And to put herself in this great danger? They say she was accused of carrying mail here? Was this the first time she committed this terrible impudence?*

 *The rest of the letter is completely personal. It was dated 9/10/44 and arrived in an O.H.M.S. envelope...so I suppose it was brought over personally + has probably been through some sort of organization, if not yours!*

 *I am prepared to tell him that all will be explained to him later on... + suggest him trying the French Red X for parcels. In a P.S. he adds that he has been under surveillance by the Gestapo for a long time. I didn't send any message to Mrs. Lefort by the Red X in the end, it didn't seem worth the awful risk to her of adding evidence of connection with their country. If you can suggest any method, or do anything, to help please tell me, as I fear it's hopeless under the circumstances. Dr. Lefort's estimation of my powers of influence is an illusion! Much as I would like to give help + support to both of them.*

*Yrs. Sincerely,*

*M. M. B. Graham (Mrs. R. A. Graham)*

L: At this point, of course dear Cicely, you were in ill health and imminent danger at Ravensbrück. Even in the way these papers look now, I find so much contrast between the visual perception of these correspondents and your actual dire condition.

The letters I hold are bundled with purple yarn lapped around the edges all stacked in this file, while what was happening in that real time was so not playful like purple and yarn.

Believe this or not, though, there is still more drama to come. To be quite blunt and honest, your death, or rumors of your death, creates a whirlwind of confusion. Even now, I'm still fitting the pieces together. For example, how this is not the first nor the last time Kitty makes reference to the personal nature of her correspondence between Alix and Vera Atkins. It seems that Kitty is in on to much, shall I say inside information, about you and Alix, and that she has been a life long confidante for both of you in your marriage. Are you sure you're ready to hold up for the rest of the story?

CL: Ready? Perhaps not. But yes, I would like even more clarity, especially on that theme of closure. It is necessary to me now, in order for me to let go and to embrace the past as well as the future. So, in fact yes, I am ready. Carry on.

L: Though death is drawing nigh, that is not the end of discovery for those left on earth. As you will see from this letter, passion for a cause can be an obstacle to the bigger picture.

Here is the memo posted on February 8, 1945:

*To: REC/FR/682 Capt. N. Fraser-Campbell, F.A.N.Y. PARIS*
*From: Flt/O. Atkins, LONDON.*
*Mrs. Cicely M. LEFORT*

*Dear Nancy,*
*I should be most grateful if you would get in touch with this lady's husband Dr. Alix LEFORT of 28 Avenue Bosquet, Paris. He knows that his wife was arrested at MONTÉLIMAR and he knows the camp in which she is now interned i.e. Frauen-Konzentrations-Lager, Ravensbrück bei*

*Furstenberg, Mecklenburg. He has been sending parcels
to her regularly but now apparently has run short of stuff
to put in them. I should be grateful if you could supply
from stock anything he may want. Personally I hope it
will be too late to reach her.*

*I think you will find him fairly indignant about the
work which she has undertaken to do which he qualifies as
dangerous and absurd, and I think a very frank discussion
with him would be helpful. I should also be glad if you
would confirm with him that she is still in the above
mentioned camp. Please let me know the outcome.*

*Yours,*
*Vera*


L: And sometime soon, dear and lovely Cicely, as we have already
documented, you are simply gone.

CL: Let's be realistic, then, and title the rest "postmortem."

L: As you wish.

# III. POSTMORTEM

Des Moines, Iowa *Tribune* May 7, 1945 front page
*Author's collection*

**L: DEAR CICELY.** Before I continue with the necessary acceptance of your death, I feel I should insert a detail of irony that involves the death of another participant in this saga. I hate to even utter the name, for this man's existence represents the most evil side of humanity. However, to be realistic, the person who went by the name Hitler entered his death realm on April 30, 1945. He was a coward, and rather than face the truth of his failure, he took his own life, and the life of his bride, Eva Braun.

I know, dear. This date would have been your 45th birthday, but due to Hitler's delusional influence on his followers, you were no longer living on this earth.

CL: Forgive me, but I have no words.

L: I understand. I will continue, somberly, with your own dreadful demise.

*1 June 45*
*To: Flt/O.V. ATKINS*
*From: Captain HAZELDINE*
*Madame LEFORT*

> *On receipt of your telegram yesterday we wrote to Dr. LEFORT breaking the news of his wife's death as gently as possible, and asking him for an appointment to go and see him and talk things over. The next thing we knew was that Dr. LEFORT's maid (an aged retainer) called at the Cécil Hôtel during the afternoon to say that she had intercepted the letter as Dr. LEFORT was due to go away for a weekend's rest, and would break the news to him on his return. Further she brought in the letter of which we are sending you a copy, which was addressed to her by Madame Gorce Boussiere, who apparently knew Madame Lefort in Germany. It seems that this dear old maid has been conducting an enquiry on her own and has apparently been successful in contacting someone who knew Madame Lefort intimately and was with her up to the end. Dr. Lefort is not aware of these "démarches" yet.*

*"COPY OF LETTER HANDED TO US BY DR. LEFORT'S MAID"*
*(see overleaf)*

*27 mai 1945*

> *Mademoiselle, excuse the late response to your letter, but I have had a bad fever since my return. I am just now feeling a little better. I knew very well Mrs. Lefort. I considered her among my friends and appreciated her simple courage.*

> *We were separated the 13th of January. People regularly suffering and the aged women... She had lost a lot of weight, having a big wound in her back, but despite this she carried herself very well (for the camps). We all wanted more food than was allowed.*

> *The first few days of May seven comrades came back. Mrs. Lefort was called one morning by name, with Miss Young and Madame Levasseur. They had numbers marked with lanolin on their arms. After that we never saw them again.*

> *Don't give up hope. We have cried and were scared for ourselves that our unfortunate friends were submitted to this terrible end. On the other hand I don't want to be naïve. But I would like for her to come back among us, if ever you hear something happy on the subject.*

*Madame Gorce Boussiére.*
*(Nelly Gorce 65 Avenue des Etats Unis. Thiers, Puy de Dôme)*

L: May 29, 1945, your earnest husband, Dr. Alix Lefort, receives this letter:

*Dear Sir,*

> *It is with the greatest sorrow that I have to inform you of the death of your wife in the Ravensbrück camp. As you know she had been a volunteer for a very dangerous and important mission in France in 1943 that she carried out very well.*

> *Her bravery and dedication have greatly contributed to the quick liberation of southern France and we have been very proud of her faithful and devoted collaboration.*

*So far we have not any detailed information but we hope*
*to have soon possible evidence from one of her friends who*
*took refuge in Sweden and we will pass on every information*
*we can get.*

*Colonel Roger with whom she worked in the Montélimar*
*area, asked me to send you his most heartfelt condolences and*
*my staff and I send you, dear Sir, our deepest sympathy in*
*your tragic loss.*

Colonel Maurice Buckmaster

L: Vera writes this memo on June 5, 1945:

*To: Captain HAZELDINE*
*From: Flt/O. ATKINS*
<u>*Madame LEFORT*</u>

*Thank you for your P/FH/463 of 1st June. I am still*
*waiting confirmation and further details from SWEDEN*
*and will let you have these as soon as received.*

*We are not taking steps to have her officially posted*
*as a casualty until this further evidence is obtained. In the*
*mean time there appears to be no doubt that she was killed*
*by being sent to the gas chamber.*

*Vera*

L: Docteur Lefort uses his formal letterhead to write the message
below. Upon receipt at SOE, this letter is written upon in English with
pencil in the margin and circled with blue pen "Missing Agents." In red
pencil marked at the top is written "Extracted from PARIS files," and
in larger print with lead pencil the code reference L23 has been
added. Alix dated this 5.VI.45:

*Madame,*

*This is horrible news to confirm what I suspected by*
*the deportation along with people I had written to, or*
*seen. I don't know exactly how my poor wife who has*
*sacrificed her life for her country is dead. Did she die from*
*a wound? Or was she killed by infamous Germans? Since*

*yesterday, with courage and high morals this detention of a martyr.....that she was dead and killed with a young Scottish person, Miss Young, and Miss Levasseur. She was evacuated to a camp for sick people where she never returned. I hope that you would telephone me to visit at 1:15 – 2:00. I am always at my house. I thank you for your letter and the sentiments for my dear (wife). She came from an old English family, Lord Granville Gordon and is the niece of the Marquis of Huntley.*
*Dr Lefort*

L: Two days later, Alix writes another letter, to Colonel Buckmaster. Apparently he kept different stationery at each office, as the printed headers differ. The letter two days ago seemed to come from his Ave. Bosquet office, and this one seems to have been written at *Maison de Sante,* the *Clinique Saint-Raphael. Docteur* must have been at hospital:

*7 June 1945*

*Monsieur, In my unbelievable pain your letter gave me a little bit of comfort and especially pride. She voluntarily accepted a dangerous mission and she must have accomplished her duty with courage and an intractable will. England and France can be proud of her. She did not know on this earth the pleasure of seeing the victory to which she contributed. She profoundly loved her country — since June 1940, certainly England was in danger. She left everything in France to be among her compatriots, and to help her country from the invaders.*

*She was from a large Scottish family where honor never failed and she's a testimony to courage of great people. I want your King to approve of what she did for a cause of the Allies. Would you have the goodness to relay to Col Roger my thanks for his thoughts, and to ask him if at all possible, that her heroic acts be recognized. I am so proud of her. Please accept, Colonel, my high considerations.*
*Dr. A Lefort*

L: And here, Cicely, is this moving response to Alix, from Francis Cammaerts:

*5 July 1945*

> *Dear Dr. Lefort. Words are so useless. How may I express the sorrow I felt when I heard of the death of Mrs. Lefort. I was so proud to have the privilege to work with her. We were battle companions. Her bravery and dedication would have been regarded as very exceptional even for a man.*
>
> *Without her, during many months, I should not have been able to do anything. She was my right arm. She also saved my life because when she was arrested she remained very discreet and the Germans never knew what she was doing.*
>
> *You must be very proud of her. I know you are. Alas! I cannot go on. Please do believe in my great emotion and in my friendship. No words can reduce the suffering.*
>
> *I share your sorrow very sincerely and deeply. Her bravery is very well known over here and I can assure you that everybody has the impression to have lost a sister.*

*Yours truly,*
*Francis Cammaerts*

L: Six weeks go by. Then Kitty sends this letter to Colonel Buckmaster:

*17 July 1945*
*Dear Colonel Buckmaster.*

> *I am writing to ask if you can give me the necessary information to help Dr. Alix Lefort, of 28 Avenue Bosquet, Paris VII e, husband of my cousin, the late Cicely M. Lefort who worked under your dept. He has written to enquire how he can get some sort of official confirmation of her death in Ravensbrück Camp, about which you wrote to him early in June (or late in May). Some death certificate is required for legal purposes with regard to Mrs. Lefort's will and also Dr. Lefort wishes to have a funeral mass in Paris.*

*Matters are unbelievably complicated and the first
step is official confirmation of death. Please, if you can,
tell me how to set about it. Mrs. Lefort was of French
nationality by marriage, tho' British by birth. She died in
a concentration camp for political prisoners after working
over here in the W.A.A.F and under your orders. To what
authority, French or English, does one apply?*

*I did have correspondence with Major I.K. Mackenzie,
12/8/44, on getting news of Mrs. Lefort's arrest through a
Red X. message from Dr. Lefort, so am addressing this letter
in a way which I hope will reach you, but please excuse
errors, as I only had your name and "War Office, Hotel
Victoria" from Dr. Lefort, and forgive my troubling you.*
*Yrs sincerely,*
*M.M.B.Graham (Mrs. R.A. Graham)*


L: Another week passes. A letter regarding "Mrs. Cicely Margot
Lefort, decd.," is sent to Colonel M. J. Buckmaster, War Office, Hotel
Victoria, Northumberland Avenue:

*Lloyds Bank Limited*
*Executor & Trustee Department*
*5, Albemarle Street,*
*London, W.I.*
*25 July, 1945*

*Dear Sir, We have been advised of the death in
Ravensbrüch Camp in Germany of the above mentioned
lady who whilst in England executed a Will under which
she nominated this Bank Executor and Trustee. The
document is dated the 15th August 1940 and we have yet
to ascertain whether, as Mrs. Lefort was by marriage a
French subject, the Will is effective. We have reason to
believe, however, that she may have made a Will of a later
date and our purpose in writing is to enquire whether you
hold any papers on her behalf or whether you can tell us of
anybody with whom we may get in to touch who may*

*have received papers from her shortly before her death. We*
*should be glad of any information and assistance which*
*you can give us and in writing will you kindly tell us*
*whether we can obtain an official Certificate of death for*
*you should it be necessary for us to have one.*
*Yours faithfully,*
*(signature) pro Manager.*

L: July 28, 1945 RAVENSBRÜCK (this is testimony, dear Cicely, recorded by your faithful ally Vera Atkins):

*I saw Mary LINDELL DE MONCY on 15 June 1945 at St. Ermine's Hotel. She struck me as being a reliable informant*:

1.  Cicely LEFORT

Some time after she arrived as RAVENSBRÜCK, Cicely LEFORT had to undergo an operation. This was done by Dr. TREITE who made a very good job of it. She continued to receive better diet for two or three months afterwards. She was never really strong. Some time in November or December 1944 the JUGENDLAGER was opened and was supposed to be a convalescent home for inmates from the main camp. Actually women who were sent there because of their failing health were generally gassed or killed by hypodermic syringes if they did not make a quick recovery. They were however not required to work and this appealed to many. Approximately in January Cicely LEFORT and an Englishwoman by the name of Mary O'SHAUNESSY were sent to the JUGENDLAGER. When Mary DE MONCY heard of this she sent them messages instructing them to volunteer to return. Mary O'SHAUNESSY took this advice and was eventually liberated but Cicely LEFORT decided to stay with another Englishwoman, I believe Mary YOUNG. Anyhow according to Mary DE MONCY, Cicely LEFORT and this other Englishwoman were given the hypodermic in early March 1945.

2.  Danielle, Violet, Odette and Lilian

Arrived in RAVENSBRÜCK in the Summer of 1944. Were sent on transport (I believe in October 44 to TORGAU) and returned to

RAVENSBRÜCK. They were again sent on transport, this time to Little KONIGSBERG and returned towards the end of January 1945. Some time at the beginning of February they were moved to the Strafblock and from there to the Bunker. She does not know what became of them. It is possible that Geneviève DE GAULLE may know.

L: July becomes August, and activity surrounding the death of Cicely picks up. (Stay with me, Cicely.)

Alix writes a brief letter, on yet another form of stationery from his Avenue Bosquet address, a smaller piece of paper, as if torn from a memo or prescription pad:

2 *August 1945*

> *Monsieur, In your letter dated 24 May 1945 when you announced the good conduct and heroism of my wife, you mentioned some who are witnesses to her death and by her colleague who went to Sweden. These women are in England. I would like to have information and some details of her last moments. As witnesses this is indispensible to me as an official act of death.*

L: Vera writes to Alix. This letter is typed in French. Was Vera fluent in French, in the written word as well as verbal translations? It makes sense that a woman of her aptitude would have this ability.

CL: Ahem. Yes dear. Allow me to intercede for a moment. Vera was more than fluent. She spoke at least three languages quite proficiently, a forte I was impressed to discover during our numerous encounters.

L: Indeed, it served her well, as you may now witness:

18 *August 1945*

> *Cher Monsieur, Colonel Buckmaster asked me to respond to your August 2 letter. We are still trying to obtain other details, especially the date of death for*

*Madame Lefort as necessary measures to obtain an official declaration of death.*

*Once we have received the necessary information, this declaration will be made by the Air Ministry of Britain for Madame Lefort's dependants.*

*Yours faithfully,*

L: August 18, 1945 was a busy day for Vera's correspondence. She sends this brief note to The Manager at Lloyds Bank Ltd at 5 Albemarle St. in London:

*Dear Sir,*

> Mrs. Cicely Margot LEFORT
> 
> *Whilst it is to be feared that this lady died in the camp of RAVENSBRÜCK, we have not so far been able to obtain sufficient information to enable us to take casualty action.*
> 
> *Further enquiries are in hand, and I will revert.*

*Yours faithfully,*

L: August 18, 1945. This, from Vera to Kitty on War Office stationery. also identified and signed V.M. Atkins, leading Kitty to also believe that V.M is a man:

*Dear Mrs. Graham,*

> *I am afraid that no official confirmation of Mrs. LEFORT's death is yet obtainable. I am still trying to obtain more details, particularly as to date and cause of death.*
> 
> *I am very sorry for this delay, but it is inevitable in this very complicated case. Yours sincerely,*

*V.M.A.*

L: And then, much like the Red X messages between Alix and Cicely (yes, Cicely, I trust that I still have your audience), on August 20, Kitty writes a reply on this same piece of paper and mails it back to V.M. Atkins. Documents pass very quickly now that the war is

over, and especially this correspondence that passes only between
districts in London:

> Many thanks — Dr. Lefort has now been advised by
> the French authorities that they will write a death certificate
> if he can obtain certain statements from 3 women at
> Ravensbrück who saw his wife alive and knew that she
> was removed to the house outside the camp on a certain
> date + was not seen alive again after that.
>
> It would be an enormous help if you could produce a
> copy of the statements made by a Mme Sylvia Rousselin
> to the Br. Consulate official who came to visit her + other
> women from Ravensbrück for details about Mrs. C.M.
> Lefort after their release in Sweden. I am trying to trace
> Mme Rousselin somewhere in Scotland as she can give
> the evidence required + said in a paper that Br. Consulate
> officials from Stockholm interviewed her. If so I expect
> you have their report + being official it would help Dr.
> Lefort. All his l.s.d. (Lloyds Bank) is still blocked!

With my apologies,
Yrs. Sincerely,
M.M.B.Graham

L: Here is what appears to be an internal SOE memo:

To: DS. From F. (Mr. Lloyd)
Mrs. C. LEFORT
23rd August, 1945

> You very kindly promised this morning to pass on to
> our representative in STOCKHOLM some enquiries into
> the presumed death of one of our agents at RAVENSBRÜCK.
> The facts are as follows:
>
> Mrs. LEFORT was imprisoned at RAVENSBRÜCK,
> and in telegram No. 496 from Stockholm of the 28th May we
> were informed that a certain Elisabeth SMITH released from
> RAVENSBRÜCK had stated that Madame LEFORT had
> been gassed and burnt in the JUGENDLAGER. Further

*information has been provided by Cicely LEFORT's aunt, who has informed us that three women gave details to the British consular officials who visited them in Sweden. One of these women was a Mrs. Sylvia ROUSSELIN, who is now believed to be somewhere in England. I presume that a copy of her statement could be obtained from the Consular officials at STOCKHOLM and it is particularly necessary to have this in order to establish Mrs. LEFORT's death. The French officials are prepared to issue a death certificate if this statement can be obtained, in order that the usual executive formalities can be carried out in winding up her estate.*

L: Cicely! How are you doing with all this? Do you see what commitment is going on to verify and establish your service and sacrifice? The dots to be connected, the lines to be crossed, the mysteries to be solved? There will still be more unexplained notes, dear one, and I will be asking more of you as we continue. Like your cousin Kitty (sometimes misidentified by other chroniclers as your aunt), I already apologize for worrying you, but yes, it is necessary. And you see, you did not simply disappear, for much effort has developed so that your life is not one of those that got lost in the aftermath of this war. Why, even now!

I understand why you are not quite up to conversation at the moment. Yes, that can wait, and I will continue to report all of this postmortem correspondence. In the midst of these many intentions to confirm your death (your murder!), the next document is a recommendation for you to be made a Member of the Most Excellent Order of the British Empire (MBE). It happens to be almost one year since you were first arrested. You are highly regarded and your sacrifice is hereby acknowledged:

*14 September, 1945, action signed by C. McV. Gubbins, Major-General*
*This officer (C.M.Lefort) was landed in France by aircraft in June 1943 as courier to an important circuit in the South East. She worked with tireless energy and devotion for three months, often in conditions of grave danger and rendered valuable assistance to her commanding officer.*

*She travelled extensively throughout South Eastern France carrying messages to the various groups of the organisation and showed great coolness and presence of mind in passing many police controls.*

*On the 10th September 1943, S/O LEFORT was arrested by the Gestapo. Although severely interrogated and ill-treated she gave no vital information away. She was last heard of in a concentration camp in Germany, and is still missing.*

*For her courage, perseverance and devotion to duty it is recommended that this officer be appointed a Member of the Order of the British Empire (Military Division).*

L: September 23, 1945. Here, Cicely, is a letter from Franklin Humble's sister, Christobel. This is the first I know of her, but she too is concerned about you:

*Dear Colonel Crockett,*

*I don't know if you remember who I am, but I worked for you for a short time at the War Office in 1940.*

*I hope you will forgive me for bothering you, but we are very anxious to get some information about a cousin of ours Cicely Lefort, and I don't quite know who to get in touch with.*

*Cicely Lefort was sent to France at the end of 1943 and was working for the War Office. We have not heard from her since then, but have just heard from my brother in Canada who says he has heard that she was arrested by the Germans and sent to a camp at Ravensbrück at the beginning of this year, and that she is supposed to have been gassed there.*

*I don't know where he got this from, but if there is any means of finding out what has happened to her, I should be so grateful to you if you would let me know.*

*Yours sincerely,*

*Christobel Humble.*

L: September 27, 1945. A follow-up and response to Christobel's enquiry, for some reason stamped in large red block letters at the top: SECRET. "They" apparently haven't been part of any of your investigation, as they refer to you, Cicely, as Miss. This paper comes out of the War Office, Whitehall, and is addressed to:

*S/Ldr. H.E.Park, SOE*

*Dear Park,*
*       As spoken, I now send you copy of a letter received by Brig. Crockett...from a former employee, Miss Christobel HUMBLE, enquiring as to the fate of her cousin, Miss Cicely LEFORT, who I understand was a W.A.A.F. officer.*
*       I have informed _____ that I have passed this to you for enquiries through the Air Ministry, and that you or they will contact Miss HUMBLE direct as to the result.*
*Yours sincerely,*

L: On October 2, 1945, Vera sends this message to Christobel at 65 Princes Park Avenue, N.W.11:

*Dear Miss Humble,*
*       Your enquiry of September 23, 1945 addressed to Colonel Crockett about your cousin Mrs. Cicely Lefort has been passed to me.*
*       We have been in correspondence with Mrs. Graham as well as with Dr. Lefort. The latest information we have is certainly most distressing. It is that Mrs. Lefort was sent to a small camp near Ravensbrück in February 1945, and it is believed that she was gassed. There is however no confirmation of this report and we are still trying to obtain further evidence before taking casualty action.*
*I am very sorry to have to pass you this sad news.*
*Yours sincerely,*
*V.M.A.*

L: October, and the search continues for a definitive answer to how you died, Cicely. Vera, I believe, also writes this memo, perhaps

to Air Ministry, on the same day that she wrote to Christobel with
the unfortunate news:

> *2 October, 1945*
>> *It has not been possible to obtain a reliable or eye
>> witness account of this lady's death in RAVENSBRÜCK.
>> I very much fear that she was in fact gassed or killed by
>> an injection in late February or early March of this year
>> in the JUGENDLAGER.*
>>
>> *I have read numerous reports on the camp and have
>> interviewed several persons returned from there of whom
>> the most reliable are Flt/O Y. BASEDEN and an
>> Englishwoman known as Marie LINDELL DE MONCY.
>> While she herself feels certain that our friend was killed,
>> she has absolutely no proof of it.*
>>
>> *I am hoping shortly to obtain a report on the
>> interrogation of some of the Rav. guards, and I should like to
>> await this report before taking further action. If this should
>> also prove inconclusive I think we should post her as "missing
>> presumed killed" in February/March 1945 and assume death
>> six months after this casualty action has been taken.*
>>
>> *I can see no reason why her citation for the M.B.E
>> should not go forward. The citation was prepared prior to
>> any report being received of her death.*
>>
>> *Do you agree with these views?*

L: October 2 was a busy day for letter writing. Alix also writes a
letter on this day, addressed to V.M. Atkins. His handwriting is taking
on an anxious presentation, as if he is losing patience with this
continued process. And it looks as if Vera or someone in the English
office took a pencil and corrected Alix's mistake of V.F. Atkins by
marking an M over the F, and also circling Monsieur, recognizing
that Alix believes V. is a man:

> *Dear Monsieur, I write again as to the act of death of
> my poor wife who died in February at Ravensbrück. I
> think now that you have been told that I am researching*

*the date in order to establish an act by the Ministry of Air
Britanique. It is absolutely necessary for French affairs to
set straight and cannot wait any longer. I am infinitely
grateful if you would do all you can to establish this act,
even though it is really painful.*

L: October 10, 1945, Vera types (it was in French) a letter to Alix:

*Dear Sir, I received your letter of 2 October 1945
concerning the death of Madame Lefort. After gathering
all the information, there is almost no doubt that she died
in the Jugendlager... though there is still no formal proof
to establish this act of death.*

*We continue our research but are worried that we
might not establish this act of death. The action we can
report is "Missing, believed killed." If there is no more
definitive news about her death, after a certain time, the
act of death will be formally established.*

*I understand the difficulties of your situation but there is
no way to behave differently in these sad circumstances.*
Faithfully yours,

L: In-house memo, typed by Vera, concerning you, Cicely, as
C. Lefort:

*23 October, 1945*
*...I should be obliged if you would confirm to me in
writing that we can post the above as "missing presumed
killed" and that if we do so death will not be definitely
assumed for a further period of six months.*

*I am very much afraid that it may take several more
months before we can obtain further evidence, and we
cannot of course be certain of ever obtaining it. I am
therefore anxious to take action on the information now
available and to assume death six months after the date of
this action provided no further information comes to light
in the meantime.*

*I feel that the safeguard of not assuming death for a
further six months is particularly necessary in this case as
this lady's husband, Dr. Alix Lefort, is anxious to enter
into possession of her funds and to remarry. I feel under
no obligation to help him in this, but on the contrary am
inclined to take every possible precaution to prevent it
whilst there is still the slightest chance that Mrs. Lefort
may be alive.*

L: And so Vera's investigation continues, with letters to the women
who knew you, Cicely, from your alarming time at Ravensbrück. To
think that there really was some slight possibility that you might
have survived!

CL: As I feel right now, I will be so bold as to say I'm not so sure
I would have wanted to survive. What would I have had to look
forward to? It does seem, in light of all that has come down since this
time, it was quite a bit of benefit that I did not return. Sad, perhaps,
but true, and I mean it sincerely, not as a ploy for sympathy
whatsoever. I'd like to see, now, what my friends had to say about
my suspected demise.

L: October 24, 1945, Vera types, in French, a letter to Sylvia
Rousselin at 103 rue Erlanger, Paris:

*Dear Madame, Dr. A. Lefort gave me your address to
know details of Madame Cicely Lefort. You might have
information about the possible dates and circumstances
about what happened to her.*
　　*I will write to Madame Chatenay and to Madame
Renaud of St. George and any other persons who knows
what happened to Madame Lefort. I regret having to ask
for such information of a good friend...*
*Faithfully yours,*

L: Two days later, Vera writes the same letters, also both in
French, to Mme Chatenay at Saint-Barthélemy-d'Anjou, near Angers,

and to Mme Renaud at 41 rue Mirabeau in Paris. This same day, she also types a letter to Alix (misspelling his name as Alex):

> *26 October 1945*
>> *Dear Sir, I received your letter of 23 October, and am grateful for the names and addresses which you provided me. I have written to them asking for details about the circumstances of Madame Lefort.*
>> *You will receive official notification of Madame Lefort as "missing" unless the details leave no doubt that is necessary to establish all we need to say that she died in order to obtain a death certificate.*
>> *If there exists even a little bit of doubt, her death will not be assumed for 6 months, that being April 1946.*
> *Faithfully yours,*

L: And here is the letter Alix wrote to Vera three days prior, on October 23, the one she refers to above:

> *23 October 1945*
> *Dear Sir, I received your letter dated 10 Oct, 1945.*
>> *…It is absolutely indispensable for my affairs to obtain this official act of death to begin life in France again. I must leave at noon to go to the middle of France for I am not wanting to stay here any longer. I can't do anything without this act of death, and this prejudgment against me. I am absolutely certain that my poor wife is deceased. All the proof has been affirmative. I am asking you to seek the formal testimonies …here are the addresses…to designate other than "missing, believed dead." How much time in order to say this act of death is established?*

L: On November 7, Vera receives a reply from Mme Chatenay on letterhead from La Romanerie, Saint-Barthélemy-d'Anjou, Angers. Contrary to the results Alix was hoping for, this letter only seems to add fuel to Vera's fire, and support her efforts to proceed cautiously with any death confirmation:

*Dear Sir. In answer to your letter dated 26 Oct. I did know Madame Cecile Lefort very well at Ravensbrück, + I was in block 11 with her when she received the letter from her husband informing her that he was divorcing her. It was a terrible blow for her + she made a new will the next day annulling the will made in favour of her husband that she had made in London. I believe it was witnessed by a doctor + perhaps two of the nurses in block 11. Madame Lefort was I believe taken to the Jugendlager but that I cannot certify to. She did not come with me to Sweden + I have not seen her since some where about February last. I still hope that she will turn up, as I believe there are still some political prisoners in Russia.*

*Believe me, Yours sincerely,*
*B. G. Chatenay*

L: You realize, dear Cicely, that every scrap of note concerning you is here in this stack of papers that I have copies of. These documents seem to very much keep your story alive and breathing. Here is a handwritten note from Christobel to Vera, nothing revealed. But still, it is a symbol of how much you were loved:

*4th November, 1945*
    *Thank you very much for your letter of 2nd October and I must apologize for not answering it before. We have heard from Mrs. Graham about Mme Lefort + no doubt shall get the whole story from her shortly....*
*Yours sincerely,*
*Christobel Humble*

L: Agh. There's the first reference to Kitty knowing "the whole story." Please, Cicely, will you not fill in the blanks?

CL: I am too tired. Let's just continue, and see what filters down. *Je vous en prie.* I beg of you.

# DEVOTED TO YOU

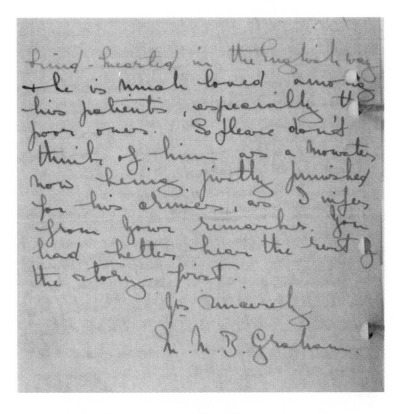

SOE file, "The rest of the story" letter from Kitty to Vera.
*Dr. David Murphy*

**L: WE'RE SOON TO SEE** just how devoted Vera was to you, perhaps to a point of prejudice against Alix, to be sure. And, I suppose the following letter hints to the innate *manqué d'amour* between the English and the French. Here is a memo Vera wrote on November 13:

> *I attach a copy of a letter received from Madame Chatenay in response to my enquiry. Dr. Lefort had given her name as one of the persons who could confirm that Mme Lefort had died in the Jugendlager of Ravensbrück. You will see that not only is this not confirmed but that the witness in question feels there is still hope that she may be alive; personally I do not share this hope to any extent.*
>
> *I feel that the existence of the will made by this lady (Mrs. C. Lefort) in Ravensbrück should be taken into account when the day comes for settling up her affairs, and therefore that it is important that a copy of the attached letter should find its way on to her files.*

L: November 16, three days after the above memo, the officer responsible for the French Section's records, Group Captain Redding, declares this perspective, but to whom it is not clear. This is also a clue as to the time of post-war activities, when records would be sealed and offices closed:

> *In view of the fact that my Section will shortly be closing down I feel that any information we receive concerning casualties to our people should be in your hands.*
>
> *The above named officer (A.S.O.C. Lefort, 9900) is still missing and I am afraid there is not much chance of her being found. Her husband, who appears to be rather a nasty piece of work, is most anxious to prove her death, so that he can get probate of her Will.*
>
> *It now appears that a woman who was in the same prison witnessed a Will made whilst in prison, annulling the one which she made in favour of her husband in London. I attach a copy of the letter from this woman and shall be grateful if you will attach it to Lefort's file.*

> *For your information I have ascertained that her*
> *husband was going to divorce her on grounds of desertion*
> *because he considered that her joining the resistance*
> *movement might endanger his own wretched life.*

L: That is painful to read, dear Cicely. When I first saw this, it felt like such an affront, and I am so thankful that we have your dear cousin Kitty's interpretation on all of these matters. But by now all avenues are being exhausted, and finality is closing in. The Accounts Department is clearing files as well:

> *November 20, 1945*
> *The above named officer must now be presumed*
> *missing, and it is requested that the usual casualty action*
> *be taken and that she may be posted away from service…May*
> *1, 1945.*
> *Pay at a consolidated rate has been issued by us up to*
> *and including April 30, 1945, and no over issue has*
> *occurred. The following particulars apply….*

L: The memo goes on with the particulars, none of which seem to reveal more, except perhaps that this document, too, is signed by Group Captain Redding. So, perhaps it was not Vera (or not Vera alone?) who held such (British) contempt for Alix.

15 November 1945, Sylvia Rousselin sends a reply to Vera's earlier letter. She says that she has transmitted the details to one Miss Myriam Humble and that she agrees with what Madame Chatenay knows of Madame Lefort.

And three days later, Monday November 18th, Mme Chatenay writes another letter to Vera, still thinking V.M. is a man, as it is addressed to:

> *Dear Sir:*
> *I am afraid that Madame Cicely Lefort is dead but as*
> *I told you before, I lost sight of her when she went to the*
> *jugendlager—but that is no proof of death as many came*
> *back—she certainly made a will in favour of some English*

*relations the day after she received the letter from her husband—It was a great shock to her as she had no idea that he wanted a divorce, + in the circumstances she was unable to defend herself. As we all felt doubtful about surviving the ordeal of Ravensbrück Cicely decided at once to make a new will. I was not able to see her for two or three days, being in trouble myself and having to work 13 hour days + I am not sure who witnessed the will nor who kept it, but I am sure that in it she disinherited her husband. I do hope that you will let me know if you do learn anything definite about Cicely—*

*I remain, yours sincerely,*

*B. G. Chatenay*

L: On November 29, Vera then sends a brief note to Christobel:

*Dear Miss Humble,*

*I have now received a letter from Madame Sylvia Rousselin saying that she has sent to you all the information she has on Mrs. Cicely Lefort. I should be glad if you would let me have a copy of Madame Rousselin's letter to you.*

L: This same day, Vera writes to Kitty:

*Dear Mrs. Graham,*

*With reference to our previous correspondence concerning Mrs. Cicely Lefort. I feel bound to bring to your notice a letter which I have recently received from a French lady who had become very friendly with Madame Lefort in the camp of Ravensbrück. This letter, of which I attach a copy, throws a new light on the question of settling up our poor friend's estate. I had heard from various sources that the communication she received from Dr. Alix Lefort caused her very deep distress and greatly undermined her morale. In the light of this knowledge, I am afraid I view the present inconvenience to which Dr. Lefort is put with some indifference.*

>*We shall continue to make very careful investigations and I will keep you informed.*
>
>*Yours sincerely,*

L: And still the same day, November 29:

>*Ref. attached letter from Mrs. Graham to* _____. *You know my views on Dr. Alix Lefort and I think we cannot do better than refer* _____ *to your note to them dated 16ᵗʰ November, 1945. I am writing to Mrs. Graham with whom I have already been in correspondence as per copy attached. I should like your views before dispatching the original.*

L: Now it is December, 1945. Here is a brief note from Christobel to Vera:

>*Dear Mr. Atkins*
>
>*I have sent your letter on to my sister, who is away for a few days, as it was she who got in touch with Mme Rousselin, + I have asked her to send you a copy of that letter.*
>
>*Yours sincerely,*

L: Ah, so Christobel did have a sister, and that must be the Myriam Humble from above? Cicely? Do you...did you...know these young ladies? Cicely? You're fading, dear. All right, onward then, and the following letter, written by Kitty:

>*Dec. 5, 1945*
>
>*Dear Mr Atkins. Many thanks for your letter of Nov 29 + the enclosure from Mme Chatenay, which I only received this morning. Do you think you could possibly arrange to see me? even by coming to lunch with me at Brown's Hotel on any date (except Dec 14 or 11) at any time convenient to you, or if I could come to the W.D. or you to the buildings of Kensington.*

*I could tell you more in 5 mins than I can write in much longer time + I see that as you have plunged into the intimately personal investigation of my cousin Mme Lefort's affair, it is best for you to hear the whole of them. I very deeply regret that Cicely even knew about the intention of divorce as I have always hoped she was spared all that additional trouble but you must remember that her husband was in complete ignorance of her doings + that correspondence took months to get through. As always in life it is the timing of events that matter so terribly + in this case it was tragic ...*

*[there seems to be a page missing!]...other times to anyone in possession of full knowledge of events the only genuine recreation to this divorce would have been surprise that it didn't happen many years ago, + from Dr. Lefort's petition.*

*I can't quite feel your indifference to Dr. Lefort's present difficulties—if he were English he would not have them just because his wife had died, even if he had wished to divorce her. Also I know him as the only Frenchman I have ever met who can honestly be qualified as kind-hearted in the English way + he is much loved among his patients, especially the poor ones. So please don't think of him as a monster now being justly punished for his crimes, as I infer from your remarks. You had better hear the rest of the story first.*

*Yrs. Sincerely,*
*M.M.B. Graham.*

L: Vera replies to Kitty's letter and the request to meet and tell "the rest of the story":

*7 December, 1945*
*Dear Mrs. Graham,*

*Thank you for your letter of 5th December. I shall be delighted to meet you and would prefer to make it a luncheon appointment which will be less rushed. I would*

*suggest Wednesday the 12th, 1 o'clock at Brown's if that
suits you. My telephone number is ABBEY 6131. I shall be
grateful if you will confirm the appointment by telephone.*
Yours sincerely,

L: Moving on toward Christmas...I wonder what London and
Paris were like during that month (I know you can't tell me, dear
Cicely). With the war at last over, it must have been a time for great
celebration, except for Alix's restrained heart. Though torn by the
loss of your life, he must have been bursting with possibilities, and
still, immense frustration. He implores V.M. to take action:

*Paris le 21 Decembre 1945*
*Mr. V.M. Atkins (followed by 5 lines of War office address)*
    *Sir, It is really time that I must insist for a rapid
solution as to the question of <u>the act of death</u> for my poor
wife, who died at Ravensbrück in February.*
    *This act is <u>absolutely indispensable</u> for my affairs.
You know that my wife Cicely Lefort who was active in
section Officers (9.900) is dead since you wrote in a letter on
May 29 1945 "It is with profound pain that I must tell you of
the death of your wife in the camp of Ravensbrück...etc..."
Another point, I receive Benevolent Funds from R.A.F. as
pension for the reason that my wife died. All of her friends in
captivity say she left for the Jugendlager and never saw her
again. After 11 months (February 1945) since she
disappeared and 7 months since the liberation of the camp,
we can unfortunately be certain of her death.*
    *Precise details are absolutely necessary that you will send
me the official act of death. To what law can we refer to in such
unhappy cases? where one has disappeared (lost at sea)?*
    *From my side, in France, I have confided with a man
of law, and he let me know that I could get this certificate
in France—presuming the death—if you cannot announce
her death—indicating a month: February according to all
witnesses. "presumed death of Madame Cicely Lefort in
February 1945" nevertheless, even if you cannot definitively*

*announce the month as February. With this letter that you
would send me, I can obtain a certificate of death in France.*

*It would seem that this would be a normal act for the
War Office to do, considering my wife's nationality and
commitment to R.A.F.*

*For me to resume my life, I must obtain: the act of
death, and precisely the year; a letter presuming the
month this death occurred (February by all accounts).*

*I anxiously await your response, Sir, with good faith*

L: Not to be dismissed, this same day Alix has his lawyer also
write to V.A:

*Paris, le 21 décembre 1945*
*Denis Durand, Le Pres Le Tribunal Civic De La Seine*
*Aff: Lefort*
*V. Ref. FLT_O M Atkins*
*Room 238*

> *Sir, I have been hired by Dr. Alix Lefort, resident of
Paris, 28 avenue Bosquet, to obtain an official certificate
of death for Mme Cecile GORDON, his wife.*

> *Colonel M. J. Buckmaster, in his letter addressed the
29th of May 1945 to Dr. A Lefort, stated the death of his
wife in the camp of Ravensbrück.*

> *In France it is necessary to declare the month and
year of death. The companions of Mme Lefort say that she
left the camp in February 1945, and did not return.*

> *I would be grateful if on these conditions you would
address a letter to Dr. Lefort, presuming the death, but
precisely establish the month of February 1945. French
law demands a month and year.*

*Yours faithfully*

CL: So, there it is. Doctor's absolute demands, by his own hand
and that of his lawyer, on of December 21, 1945, for an official death
certificate. I wonder where Alix spent that Christmas. Probably at La
Hune. Anna would be there anyway, and no doubt, that dear young

Janine. A whole new life awaited Alix, a whole new year to begin. The war was over! I weep just imagining what a grand feeling that must have made. Oh, would that life had been fairer, that "things" had been different. But the world does indeed go on, with or without any of us.

It's still not over, is it Lizzie? I know what's to come. Maybe, just....

L: I'm feeling melancholy myself, friend. We are indeed coming to an end of some sort, although this story, the story of your life, dear Cicely, may not ever entirely end. I have one question before we do go on, and that is why would the lawyer at this last moment refer to you as Cicely Gordon, and not Lefort, especially as he was seeking your death in the context of your legal status as Alix's wife? One more mystery, I suppose. As I pointed out ages ago, or so it seems, in my future correspondence with lovely Janine Lefort she only refers to you as Cicely Gordon as well, and never Lefort.

Let us share a few more moments here together, you and I, concerning the meeting of Vera and Kitty that final Christmas season. *D'accord?*

CL: *Absolument, chére* Lizzie.

# THE FULL STORY

Memorial plaque at Ravensbrück.
*Paul McCue*

**L: CHRISTMAS HAS COME AND GONE.** It is almost the new year of 1946. But back on Wednesday, December 12 at 1:00 at Brown's Hotel, Vera and Kitty had met for lunch. Mrs. R.A. Graham (Kitty) must have called V.M. Atkins's (Vera's) office to confirm the date, and perhaps at that point, if she spoke directly to Vera, Kitty finally realized that she had been communicating all along with Vera, a woman, and not a man. I suspect a momentary hesitation, a slight gasp, followed by a stifled chuckle and finally a confession: "VERA is it? Oh my, I do feel such a fool. All along I addressed you as Sir, assuming that you were a man. I am tickled, and now look even more forward to our lunch. *Bonjour.*"

And so they met, they shared, they talked. It was at this point that the mystery of your life, your secrets, and "the rest of the story!" were all revealed. Here now is their exchange following the meeting:

*Dec 28, 1945*

> *Dear Flight Officer Atkins, I don't know if I call you that or "Miss" in a nonofficial letter! It was very kind of you to send me the photo of Cicely but I like to remember her as I last saw her when she came into my room, looking prettier than I'd ever seen her. I thought perhaps, after our meeting, you might have thought me rather heartless but these tragic things are not possible to talk about unless one treats them impersonally, + after I knew about Cicely's arrest I don't think I ever went to my comfortable bed or had a meal without thinking about her! It was so dreadful not to be able to do anything at all.*
>
> *Now I try to help Alix Lefort because I know he is a good man + he has his life to live + problems to come—if Cicely had lived I would not have taken sides with either in their personal difficulties.*
>
> *Will you let me have your private address some time in case I hear of a flat while my daughter is hunting for one. Also I can then tell you of a development in this strange saga, for your own information + interest, if there are any more.*
> *My best thanks for all your help and wishes for 1946*
> *Yrs sincerely,*
> *M.M.B.Graham*

L: Vera promptly responds to Kitty's letter:

*1 January, 1946*

> *Dear Mrs. Graham, Thank you very much for your
> letter of December 28 and your good wishes which I
> warmly reciprocate.*
>
> *I was most interested to hear the full story of Cicely's
> life and I realized your great affection for her. We shall of
> course do everything to speed up the settlement of her
> affairs but as I explained to you there is at present still
> insufficient evidence on which to take definite casualty
> action, therefore some further time will have to elapse
> before the Air Ministry Casualties Branch will consider
> taking the grave step of presuming death. In the meantime
> I am afraid there is no way in which we can help Dr. Alix
> Lefort however much we might wish to do so.*
>
> *My private address is: 725 Nell Gwynne House,
> Sloane Avenue, S.W.3, and I shall always be interested to
> hear of further developments.*

*With kind regards,*
*Yours sincerely*

L: "The full story," indeed. My fine Cicely, I think I should be
grateful that I do not know the whole story, for the opening allows
me to continue my fascination with you.

It certainly seems that one thing always leads to another throughout
such a far-reaching project. This may not have any meaning other than
coincidence, but Vera's home address is on Sloane Avenue, and I am a
Sloan. It is intriguing that, after all these years and months and pages of
research, here at almost the end, the word Sloane appears for one
time only. And had my immediate predecessors been born in
England, like yours, I would have an "e" on my surname, like Vera's
home avenue.

CL: Well then, let me enlighten you to this cultural reference
(this is rather silly!), at least as much as I am able to recall. Sloane

Square was, and I suppose it still is, a bustling station on the Tube. I do remember that colorful stop with fond regard. I can't say that Battersea Park was a particularly regular haunt for me, but it was distressful during the Blitz when Kitty and I were made aware of the significant damage inflicted.

Oh my, that memory seems to be fading, losing its hue. I'm feeling a bit subdued myself.

L: Don't fade away, Cicely. Not yet! I know, I know. It must feel as if the story has ended, but that is not to be.

CL: You're going to ask, aren't you? You do want to know what the "full story" is. You simply can't resist, even with your fascination of the unknown.

L: I can't describe my frustration when I realized that, in spite of stacks and stacks of papers documenting nearly every move you and Alix made from 1940 -1945, this one immense bit of information was not recorded, but was only transmitted person to person, ear to ear, always by word of mouth, but never on paper. And Vera was still living until only a few years ago! Had I known she was still alive…had I only known. But alas, there is this gap that I do not intend to let go. I also don't expect you to fill in "the whole story," for if you've kept this part of your life mostly to yourself (but for Kitty?) all these years, it is not up to me to insist you let it go.

CL: Reprieve. I am not ready.

L: *C'est la vie*. But still to come, finally for Alix, is the official certificate declaring your death.

The process all comes together in February 1946, one year past your disappearance. There is finally a series of letters and restricted documents to summarily report your death, in which Vera, as the Squadron Officer out of Whitehall, indeed declares you *"murdered by the Germans."*

Her five-point letter repeats the path you took, that you were in fact sent away to an extermination camp *"from which very few returned,"* and she asks for official documentation to the next-of-kin *"that casualty action has been taken on evidence which we have only now obtained."*

Vera handwrites a postscript, asking that she be permitted to write personal letters to the next of kin as soon as she hears that official notification has been sent.

At this time, because many war offices had been closed, Vera was in Germany, attached to the War Crimes Section of the Judge Advocate General's (JAG's) Branch at the headquarters of the British Army of the Rhine. She spent tireless hours tracing, locating, and meeting with every SOE agent she could find who survived the war; or as she did with you, finding every answer she could to explain and verify the deaths of those who did not return.

There is yet another curious message that Major Dalton wrote. As point two of a three-point memo, he typed: *I shall be glad if you will take the necessary casualty action with the Air Ministry, so that Miss Lefort can be notified as having met her death.*

So that *you* could be notified of your own death, indeed! Well, dear Cicely, I guess you have now been duly notified. (I note a slight smile on your weary face. Yes, humor survives.)

Finally, Lloyds Bank is officially appointed executor of the official Will you made in England. (Does this mean that the Will you made posthaste in "camp" was never found? How do you feel about that?)

And this, at last, is the letter that Alix had been seeking since the previous February:

> *Sir, I am directed to ... forward a certificate of death in respect of your wife, Assistant Section Officer C.M. Lefort.*
>
> *Such a certificate is normally accepted as proof of death by the Principal Probate Registry and will, it is hoped, meet your requirements.*
>
> *I am to state that this Department has no knowledge of the precise date of your wife's death and the 1st of May, 1945, was therefore accepted for official purposes, as the date of her presumed death.*

*If this date is not acceptable to you and you can*
*furnish written evidence that your wife died in February,*
*1945, the date of death presumption will be revised.*
I am, Sir, Your obedient Servant,

CL: Oh my dear Lizzie. You ask a good question. I do suspect that my spontaneously executed Will...suddenly I feel faint. The scene at camp...I was in no condition...no. NO. No no no no. I cannot bear to remember.

But it does seem fair enough to assume that my Will, written literally at death's door, was lost with the end of war destruction. Leave it at that, and accept this next thought: coming from where I am now, I am happy that my Will of 1940 was probate. (All service personnel were advised to submit a Will; a daunting task, but realistic.) I of course love, loved, and will always love Alix. He was my life companion. As you know well enough by now, there was another side to the story.

L: And there is another memo, dated April 25, 1946, referring to:

*A copy of a letter dated 5 March, 1946 from the husband*
*of A/S/O Lefort together with a copy of our proposed reply,*
*are forwarded for your attention. We should appreciate*
*any comments you may wish to make before a reply is*
*dispatched to M. Lefort.*

L: But I do not have a copy of Alix's letter, nor of the reply sent.

CL: Oh dear, tenacious Alix. He must have held some discontent with my certificate of death. I suspect it had to do with the date of May 1 instead of the month of February. But by now, of course, the point is moot, or useless — *inutile,* as we like to say in France.

L: It's time: Sigrún Lilja.

CL: Here we go, then. I wish you luck.

L: Sigrún knows things, as you yourself have admitted. I don't know how she does, but somehow, she does. She also has suggested, intriguingly, that you and I are more closely related than I realize. To be honest, she seems to have the gift of visions, so detailed that she was able to connect images she experienced and eventually identify you as a nurse during the First World War. When she and I first began communicating, she asked if I was sure you never had a child, for she felt certain that you did. Later, she asked again, and added that she thinks you sailed to America sometime between the wars (in the 1920s). I said that as far as I was aware, you had not. In my notes, somewhere, I recall that when I asked Janine this same question, if you ever had children, she said that Alix was quite firm about your inability to bear children.

Not long ago, quite recently in fact, Paul, the British historian who has now written a brief biography of your life, indeed sent a document that he found of a ship's manifest. He did not know that Sigrún Lilja and I had wondered about such a journey, but there was your name, traveling alone on the ship S.S. Leviathan, sailing from Southampton on December 21, 1923. You put your aunt, Mrs. Graves, who lived in Paris at the time, as your nearest relative. The destination that you listed was Cleveland, Ohio. Six months later, by June of 1924, you had returned to Paris, where on the 17th of June you and Alix walked arm in arm down the carpeted cathedral steps and out into the sunlit day as husband and wife.

Cleveland? Cicely, I don't have a clue about Cleveland. Chicago I could understand, as you and your mother had made trips to Chicago to visit your aunt, but Ohio has me clueless.

Or not. Somewhere in my meanderings through your life and your mother's life, I have come across the name Mackenzie in the ancestry line of the Close/Brooks of England, and I believe there is a branch of the family in America. Yes, full circle back to the beginning when Jimmy Close and I started to write. He mentioned the odd reference to Ireland and your use of Mackenzie as a family name. So far, though, I have not found proper leads to follow, but yes, I do wonder: Perhaps this American Mackenzie is why you chose to identify your family name as Mackenzie and not Gordon. Perhaps.

You're awfully quiet. This must be upsetting, and I do apologize. I feel that these questions deserve to be asked, even if not answered.

CL: that. history. is. so. awfully. long. ago.

I do not lie ... when I say ... that I barely remember any of it.

I have buried that time of my life into the deepest recesses of my mind.

So very, very much happened in those next years, as you can fully attest to yourself, kind Lizzie.

L: But there's more. This only recently came to light. Sigrún provided a few more thoughts concerning your solo travel to America that winter of 1923. She wrote to me:

> *Regarding Cicely and her trip to America. I think that the father of her child was British, related to a family who today is called the Windsor family, and she never told him. I think Cecily came to America, and with the help of a friend had the child. I think the person who helped her was a man possibly with the nickname Bill or Billy. He lived or had an apartment (a penthouse) in New York City and possibly a ranch in the south, maybe Texas. I also think he had horses or at least enjoyed them very much. I think he had more money than most. I also think he might have collected art work, possibly was involved with an art museum, or at least had beautiful things in his apartment. I think that he took part in WWI, and that is where Cicely met him. He did not participate in WWII. I don't think the baby was his or Alix's. I think that the child was taken care of (or given) to someone in the family.*

L: Cicely, I asked my mother about relatives we might have had in Texas. She said yes, indeed the Humbles (named Cynthia and Gretchen) did have a ranch in Texas, and she believes they had a lot of horses. There was also a wealthy cousin who lived in New York. His name was Harry, but that is all she remembers. Ohio, I still don't know.

CL: No, this is not to be. I'm sorry, but the answer is "No."
*C'est tout!* If I have no other control left to me, this is one thing
that can still be mine, and now, with everyone else gone, mine alone.

The sun must be going down, for this afternoon light is fading.
Or have we already passed into a new season? I feel so awfully tired.

But beyond my personal life saga, did the world ever understand,
ever pay attention, ever really listen to what had happened during those
dreadful years of war?

L: Many people were held accountable, Cicely. Men and women
were hanged until dead for the war atrocities committed. Dr. Treite, the
man who operated on you, was found guilty during the Ravensbrück
trials and given the death penalty, though he took a poison capsule
and died in his prison cell.

Hold on. Here is one last note from your English files, a memo
typed to Kitty from the War Office in London:

*November 27, 1946*
> *Dear Mrs. Graham, You may have read in the Press
> that the trial of the War Criminals from Ravensbrück
> Camp takes place in Hamburg on 3 Dec 46.*
>
> *We thought you would like to be informed that all
> details concerning the death of your niece have been
> placed before the Judge Advocate General's Department,
> War Crimes Section.*
> *Yours, B. E. Amos*
> *Staff Captain.*

CL: Yes, this might have been a comfort to Kitty. And look, again
I see a bit of confusion that I am referred to as Kitty's niece and not
her cousin. I do appreciate, Lizzie, how your work was certainly cut
out for you.

L: Kitty replied.

CL: Of course she did. Oh how I do miss Kitty.

L: It is a good and fair reply, Cicely. She reveals a lovely side of Alix that you were not aware of at the time, either, just as your efforts as a secret agent were not known to him:

*Dec 3, 1946*

> *Dear Captain Amos. Thank you for telling me about the Ravensbrück Camp trial + that my cousin's care has been recorded.*
>
> *I hope the newspaper reports of the escape of the two chief criminals is not true! I have seen Dr. Lefort, earlier this year, + I am glad to say that he was in the movement which helped Allied women to escape and also sheltered Jewish children in his Paris flat—its lighter side is amusing, in that he, ultra Right, joined a Communist section of the movement as it was so very much better organized. He told me that on their release from Ravensbrück he saw the wife + daughter of the man who transmitted wireless messages for, and with, Cicely + that the woman told him she had been arrested when handing in a letter to some nearest post for delivery to her husband + that he escaped when Cicely was caught.*
>
> *Dr. Lefort said his first information was that she was in prison at Toulouse, from a Belgian woman who had been there with her + then later he received a scrap of paper picked up by a railway employee saying she was being taken to Germany.*
>
> *I expect you know most of all this but it may fill in some gaps for your completion of the story.*
>
> *Thanking you again for writing.*
>
> *Yrs. Sincerely*
>
> *M.M.B.Graham*
>
> *P.S. Please note change of address, which is permanent.*

L: THERE. Cecily, there again is a reference to that ephemeral scrap of paper, tossed from the transport on your way to the death camp. But not so fleeting a scrap after all. That tossed piece of hope, written by your own hand, landed off the train (in the sweep of a frozen February scene), was picked up by some stranger's hands, delivered by who knows how many other means of transport to Alix in Paris, and actually remains, apparently intact, in a box of documents saved for you, by your husband and his second wife Janine, at that villa above the sea in St. Cast. The *coup de grâce* that would help preserve this telling of your story.

But on a lighter note, please: Some things must run in the family. This common phrase so tickles me: On December 3, 1946, Kitty Close Humble Graham wrote: *"I expect you know most of all this...."* And 56 years later, on February 13, 2002, James Humble Brooks Close wrote to me: *"I expect you know all this anyway."*

I believe that the wife and daughter that Alix mentions, those who were in Ravensbrück with you, are Auguste Deschamps's family. As an agent he was known as Albert.

Are you there? Cicely? Dear? Helloooo. You are about to receive your award!

Oh goodness. I expect you are still listening, so I will also tell you this. One of the last scraps of paper in your SOE file is merely a typed strip, accounting for the only items that remained after you "disappeared." I do so wonder where these tokens had been stored, and where they are now. The list was recorded on November 11, 1945:

1 gold ring (actually "watch" was typed, but scratched out and gold ring was written beside)
Identity card case
Personal papers
1 letter

I cannot help but imagine what that letter said. Perhaps the letter reveals the rest of the story. If the message is ever discovered, you can expect to hear from me again here, dear cousin. In the meantime, I will investigate the outcome of the MBE award that you so deserve. I understand that the award may be worn over your heart with a bow, as I will do with my memory of you!

Now let us bid adieu with this thought:

*Peut-être c'est une histoire d'amour, enfin.*
Perhaps this is a love story, after all.

# AWARDS

Poppies placed at Tangmere for Cicely by Paul McCue.
*Paul McCue*

By the KING'S Order the name of

Honorary Assistant Section Officer C.M. Lefort,

Women's Auxiliary Air Force,

was published in the London Gazette on

13 June, 1946

as mentioned in a Despatch for Distinguished

Service.

I am charged to record

His Majesty's high appreciation.

REPUBLIQUE FRANÇAISE

Guerre 1939-1945

CITATION

A L'ORDE DE L'ARMEE

A TITRE POSTHUME

LEFORT Cicely, Margot — des Forces Françaises

de l'Intérieur

AWARD

CROIX DE GUERRE AVEC PALME.

Fait à PARIS, le 14 janvier 1948

# REMERCIEMENTS

✓ Reviving Cecily Lefort's life has been an act of passion, compassion, and obsession. Each of these sentiments thrives in the positive sense of collaboration: to work with others. These forces have been in place since Cecily disappeared at Ravensbrück in 1945, and over these years have come together in the creation of *When Songbirds Returned to Paris*. I will attempt to acknowledge my allies on this journey in the order they entered my life as the researcher:

✓ I must begin with René Jamois, the enterprising Frenchman who embraced my request for information with a sense of urgency that has continued since 2003. If it were not for René's ability to make vital connections, the revival of Cecily's life would not have been possible. I cannot overemphasize this truth enough.

✓ Thérèse Dumont, a resourceful French lady, responded to the advertisement that René posted in *Le patriote résistant* in which he asked for information pertaining to the resistance network in South-East France where Cecily was dispatched. Like René, Thérèse was also 17 at the time of liberation. Nearly all of the Lefort family documents came by way of Janine Lefort to Thérèse Dumont to Réne Jamois to me. Through Thérèse, we found both Francis Cammaerts and Janine Lefort. Again, Cecily's story would be incomplete without the inclusion of these essential characters.

✓ Mrs. Alix Lefort (Janine), and her family, hold the key to the survival of the memory and honoring of Cecily's life. Not only did Janine safely store documents and photographs that record the history of the war as it affected Alix and Cecily, but for all these years following the war, she and Alix kept a photograph of Cecily on display in the family home. I regret that Janine recently passed away before I had the opportunity to meet her in person. But her daughters, Dominique, Christine, and Anne, have become important to my family thread, and the day will come when we finally meet.

⌒ Curtis Harnack's biography *Gentlemen on the Prairie,* examines the British settlers who claimed land in the American Midwest, including the Close Brothers and their various ties to my ancestors, the Humbles. Curtis became friends with my parents, as his research brought him to our doorstep to hear more about the family history, and to take a photograph of the silver House of Lords cup that Frederic Close permanently won in the 1886 June Derby. Curtis did me the immense favor of reading an early draft of Cecily's story, and responded with encouragement. Curtis, too, has since passed away.

⌒ James B. Close (Jimmy), grandson of the British settlers of Iowa, and also a relative from the Humble side, kept in regular letter writing mode with me for years, helped me understand family dynamics, sent vintage photographs, and enlightened me as to Beryl E. Escott's *Mission Improbable: A salute to the RAF women of SOE in wartime France.* As a pattern that seems all too constant, Jimmy has also crossed over the bridge of life.

⌒ Pamela A. Yenser. Friend, travel companion, fellow researcher, author, editor. Back when our friendship was still new, Pamela eased me through the hoops when, at age 50, I decided to apply to the University of Idaho Master of Fine Arts Creative Writing program (for the purpose of writing this book). Pamela joined my daughter Margot and me on the research trip to Paris in 2007. I feel honored that Pamela continues to share her infinite talent and curiosity, and I am filled with gratitude and awe for her editing abilities. Another truth: without Pamela's thoughtful insight, *When Songbirds Returned to Paris* would not be the impeccable work that I believe we have achieved.

⌒ Cecily Spiers, my Paris correspondent! When I began to plan the Paris trip, I contacted the American Graduate School of International Relations and Diplomacy (AGS) in search of a local (Paris) French translator. A student named Gabrielle replied that she "might know someone who would be able to help you." In fact, she said her bilingual American mother lived near Paris, and also "has had years of experience dealing with French bureaucracy." *Voilà!* I had my own real Cecily suddenly on this amazing journey with me. Cecily Spiers (how more perfect an identity could I hope for?) set about to organize our arrival: translating the bureaucratic paper work so I could apply to the Ministry of Defense (and making all the diplomatic arrangements), thus making me a "client" so we had access to "the individual dossier concerning the resistance activities of Mme Cecily LEFORT"; planning an evening at the American Library for a reading by author Hal Vaughan, from his book *FDR'S 12 Apostles: The Spies who Paved the Way for the Invasion of North Africa*; and locating Mrs. Riols in Marly le-Roi forest for us to meet. For payment? "2 large bottles of real vanilla extract and double-acting baking powder."

⌐ I would be remiss not to mention Pierre and Cyrill, from the *Fondation pour la Mémoire de la Déportation,* who went out of their way to accommodate strangers in a foreign land. (As an American who guiltily and regretfully lacks any functioning depth of a second language, I am beholden to those who graciously communicate at more than one linguistic level.) Margot, Pamela, and I could not have felt more welcomed, even treated as honored guests. We met, we queried, we talked. We received information, including the immediate extraction from the *Fondation* files those copies of their monthly printed bulletin that pertained specifically to Cecily, and to Ravensbrück— all in French, of course, so my understanding of their full impact has perhaps, even now, not been fully realized. Their invitation to return has not been disregarded.

⌐ Mrs. Noreen Riols. As an author, Noreen has a number of published novels based on her experiences during those years of war. Recently, after the files were made public and she no longer had to hide behind a veil of fiction, Noreen published *The Secret Ministry of Ag. and Fish: My Life in Churchill's School For Spies.* I think it's fair to say that Noreen Riols is a living legend. I am grateful for the opportunity to have been invited into her circle. Besides that endearing afternoon in her living room, Noreen kindly critiqued particular references I made, based on our interview, for accuracy and fine-tuning. She is my two degrees—the closest it is possible for me to be near the living cells of Cecily Lefort. (Noreen knew Vera, and Buck, and Francis; they each knew Cecily first hand.)

⌒ I believe Sigrún Lilja would be next. Of all connections, this was the most unexpected: to learn about a woman in Iceland who was not only also interested in Cecily's life, but was in possession of the Lefort family file as it pertained to Cecily, gave a surreal twist to my research. Sigrún generously shared information that perhaps only she was aware of, sending documents with ease through email, to save Janine from having to send copies to me through postal service, romantic as receiving those envelopes could be.

⌒ Various translators of the letters and war documents from French to English are greatly appreciated: Sarah, who spent the most time meeting with me, including a tasty tea one afternoon when my mother happened to have flown in from Iowa; visiting faculty at University of Idaho's Department of Modern Languages and Cultures; Carole, Nicolas, Monique and her lovely mother; and many others whose help has made this project possible.

⌒ Dr. David Murphy, scholar from Trinity College, Dublin. Dr. Murphy contacted me, curious about a possible Irish connection through a certain Irish ring purportedly belonging to Cecily Lefort, one of the unsolved mysteries that indeed are part of the intrigue surrounding Cecily's activities. When David anticipated an upcoming trip to London, he volunteered to stop by SOE headquarters and make copies of Cecily's entire English file. Those papers are what provided context for Part Two: What the English File Reveals. At one point during my writing, my daughter asked me which part I liked better. A tough question, and even now as I approach printing my answer, I hesitate to repeat it. I recall that I replied, "Part One; that's where the original story is. Part Two is a deconstruction of what I thought I knew, before." But without Part Two, Cicely's English files, Part One would be incomplete.

⌒ The most recent contributor to the historical accuracy of this project is Paul McCue, British historian and author. Paul contacted me during his research about Cecily—one of 13 female agents of French Section, Special Operations Executive, who did not return from the war. Paul's current project, *The Valençay 104*, is based on the 104 French Section agents who perished. His essential knowledge of SOE, the lives of agents, and particulars of the Second World War in France and England, as well as his willingness to share images, critique my narrative, and correct any factual mistakes, gives *When Songbirds Returned to Paris* a level of authenticity it would have lacked without Paul's generous contributions.

# RECONNAISSANCE

Gratitude and love goes to my parents, for their unconditional encouragement toward my passions and projects: to my father, a World War II veteran himself, who was only still living (as a feisty octogenarian) at the time when I first asked about the child who became a spy, and to my mother, for keeping track and holding on to family history, especially the prized family photograph that is the reason this entire project exists: Cecily as a child straddling her big black Chow.

I honor my sister, Margaret Humble (Meg), the third of four Margarets in this family legacy, for her steady reassurance and enduring praise.

It goes perhaps without saying, since this book is dedicated to her, but say it I shall: my daughter Margaret (Margot), the fourth in this named lineage, holds my heart and my pride. She has been a continuous source of delight on this journey we have in many ways been taking together. *Je t'adore.*

Paul Meginnis, my mother's life adventure companion, keeps a continuous look out for all things World War II as they pertain to Cecily's story, sending articles and calling with titles of books and movies for me to investigate.

Doris Fuller took time to read and comment on an earlier draft of this narrative, pushing me out of a rut that propelled me toward this final conversational technique. Doris's sincere interest in my story also inspired her to meet with Sigrún when travels took her to Iceland.

Consultations with Thornton Sully from A Word With You Press helped me set the tone and strengthened the ephemeral time aspect of this manuscript.

Finally, I am indebted to my publisher, Fawkes Press, and to Jodi Thompson for her belief in *Songbirds*. Also, to Michelle Fairbanks who provided the magnificent book cover art, and for her continued design assistance and patience for every wild idea I ask her to try; Pamela Yenser, who as my editor, rises above any expectation I could ever imagine—"overwhelmed" does not cover my volume of gratitude; Nancy Casey, whose expert proofreading provides confidence to present this book to the world; Katie Wacek, whose skill as my project manager to market *When Songbirds Returned to Paris* into far-reaching opportunities, yields enthusiastic potential.

# ABOUT THE AUTHOR

E.M. Sloan is an author and artist living in Moscow, Idaho, where she writes, makes bookart, and teaches at the University of Idaho. Elizabeth's dual UI degrees, with her undergraduate degree in art from the University of Iowa, and her Master of Fine Arts degree in creative writing from the University of Idaho, encompass stints ranging from a fine arts studio, to her graphic design business, to graphic arts at *Better Homes & Gardens*. View Elizabeth's bookarts and mixed media works at www.lizziebzArt.com, and her author's page at facebook.com/lizziebzart.

# BIBLIOGRAPHIE

## BOOKS:

Anthonioz, de Gaulle Geneviève. *La traversée de la Nuit: Recit*. Paris: Seuil, 1998. [1st French ed.] Print.

—. *The Dawn of Hope: a Memoir of Ravensbrüch*. New York: Arcade Publ. [1st English ed. of the above] 1999. Print and ebook.

Blumenson, Martin, Ed. *Liberation*. Alexandria, VA: Time-Life Books, 1978. Print.

Blumenson, Martin and Maurice Le Nan, eds. *La Libération*. Amsterdam, Time-Life Books, 1978. Print.

Escott, Beryl E. *Mission Improbable: A Salute to Air Women of the SOE in Wartime France*. Wellingborough, Great Britain: Stephens, 1991. Print.

Harnack, Curtis. *Gentlemen on the Prairie*. Ames: Iowa State UP, 1985. Print.

Irwin, Will. *The Jedburghs*. Massachusetts: U.S. Public Affairs, 2005. ebook. London: Ebury, 2006. Print.

Irwin, Will and Antoine Bourguilleau. *Les Jedburghs: L'histoire secrète des Forces Spéciales: Alliées en France en 1944*. Paris: Perrin, 2008. Print.

Marks, Leo. *Between Silk and Cyanide: A Codemaker's War, 1941-1945*. New York: The Free Press, 1998. Print. Stroud: The History Press 2013. ebook.

McIntosh, Elizabeth P. *Women of the OSS: Sisterhood of Spies*. New York: Dell, 1998. Print.

Miller, Russell, Ed. *The Resistance*. Alexandria, VA: Time-Life Books, 1977. Print.

Morrison, Jack G. *Ravensbrück: Everyday Life in a Women's Concentration Camp, 1939-45*. Princeton, NJ: Wiener, 2000. Print.

Mosley, Leonard. *Battle of Britain*. New York: Time-Life International, 1977. Print.

Mosley, Leonard; Louis Dubois, traducteur; Maurice Le Nan. *La*

*Bataille d'Angleterre.* Time-Life Books, Paris: Inter-Forum, 1977. Print.

Sommerville, Donald. *World War II: Day by Day.* Connecticut: Dorset Press [Mazal Holocaust Collection], 1989. Print.

Shirer, William L. *Berlin Diary: The Journal of a Foreign Correspondent, 1934-41.* New York: Knopf [Rouben Mamoulian Collection], 1941. Print.

Weitz, Margaret Collins. *Sisters in the Resistance.* New York: Wiley & Sons, 1995. Print.

—. *Les combattantes de l'ombre: Histoire des femmes dans la Résistance, 1940-45.* Paris: Michel, 1997. Print.

## THE FRENCH DOSSIER AND ENGLISH FILES:

Ministry of Defense. Viewed 12 March 2007, Chateau de Vincennes, Paris, France.

National Archives, London. Cecily Margot LEFORT, aka Cecile Marguerite LEGRAND, born 30.04.1900, died 01.03.1945. With photographs. Digitized record. <discovery.nationalarchives.gov.uk/details/r/C9033756>

## CORRESPONDENTS:

Close, James B.
Dumont, Thérèse
Guðbjartsdóttir, Sigrún Lilja
Harnack, Curtis
Jamois, René
Lefort family: Janine, Dominique, Christine
McCue, Paul
Murphy, David
Riols, Noreen
Spiers, Cecily

# LES IMAGES

*Au revoir,* until we meet again.
Elizabeth Sloan

# A LETTER FROM THE AUTHOR

*Dear Reader:* I hope my book, *When Songbirds Returned to Paris*, has touched you in unexpected and rewarding ways. My journey through twelve years of research and writing on this creative nonfiction narrative has been emotionally and physically exhausting. It has also been triumphant, replete with unexpected turns and surprising twists of fate, as this tragic but uplifting story of Cecily Margot Gordon Lefort—my second cousin twice removed—unfolded.

As Cecily remarks at the beginning of *Songbirds*, although war is at the heart of her life, and of my book, this story is about much more than her involvement in World War II.

The story of Cecily transcends the facts of her biography and asks you, as the reader, to participate in the perhaps quixotic life of an inspirational woman who helped turn back the tide of the Nazi regime, allowing the songbirds, both literally and metaphorically, to return to Paris.

Every day, the world loses more of our few remaining WWII veterans. Nearly every day, I come across someone whose life has been affected by this catastrophic war. Many grandparents, and now great grandparents, have come to a point in their lives when they are willing to finally talk about their memories—memories that are often painful and traumatic— stirred by this life-altering, indeed world changing, conflict.

Being the "romantic" that Cecily claims I am, my hope is that these memories include some wistful notions as well. As an artist and a writer—descended from true Romantic visionaries of the late 1800s—my instinct has been to represent emotional and intellectual aspects through this method of real, or imagined, conversations with those from our past.

I would love to hear from you with comments that include your own specific or spontaneous connections to WWII, history, family, or the transcendental process of discovery through art and story. Please follow my author's page at www.facebook.com/lizziebzart.

If you are so inclined, I would also greatly appreciate a review of *When Songbirds Returned to Paris* through any online or print venues. Book reviews will help keep this book in circulation, which in turn will keep the evidence from those "who will live to tell our stories" alive.

Thank you for reading *When Songbirds Returned to Paris*.

All the best
E.M. (Elizabeth) Sloan

*This is a work of nonfiction. To the best of the author's ability and knowledge, all characters, documents, letters, and historical content are drawn from factual research and archives. While some conversations and scenes are imagined, they are based on evidence of truth.*

# READER REVIEWS

(E.M. Sloan) skillfully interweaves facts and intrigue into a thought-provoking WWII historical account of one of England's Special Operations Executives (SOE) spies, Cecily Lefort. Supported by research, letters, photographs, and interviews, Sloan uses a creative narrative style to build a compelling tale on a personal level that immediately engages the reader.

An amazing amalgamation of scholarly level research and true feeling. The author's genuine and touching affection for a relative she's never met ushers us through one of the lesser-told dramas of World War II. This book has everything: love, mystery, loyalty, betrayal, and heroism. Good read for book clubs.

I had to keep reminding myself that is was non-fiction, because it read like a novel. I had read two books in the last few years about Ravensbrück concentration camp and about the women who were French and English spies during WWII. Both books had noted Cecily in them, and then getting to read about her entire life story was fascinating.

A splendid piece of work—boldly innovative, in places downright poetic, and a powerful biographical narrative and memoir; I found it riveting. It reminded me a bit of Julia Blackburn's *Daisy Bates in the Desert*, in that it both blends genres and takes the reader through the research process. (Stephen Preston Banks, author of *Kokio: A Novel Based on the Life of Neill James.*)

The American Library in Paris Book Award recognizes the most distinguished book of the year, written in English, on the subject of France or the French-American encounter. *When Songbirds Returned to Paris* is nominated for this 2016 Book Award.

# TOPICS FOR DISCUSSION

BIOGRAPHY:
What other books about people from the era of WWII do you recommend? How do their stories compare to Cecily's?

In what ways does the author's process of discovery about the life of Cecily Lefort inspire you to research your own family members?

HISTORY:
Does the author's technique of using dialogue between herself and Cecily successfully serve to "report" the events of her life? Why or why not?

Of the following historical periods covered in *Songbirds*, which is treated most vividly and which leaves you wanting to know more about that period: the late 1800's, the early 1900s through WWI, events leading up to and including WWII?

MEMOIR:
*Songbirds* is a blend of genres, braiding history, biography, and memoir. Are there other structures you identify in this formula of creative non-fiction?

Does this blend succeed in drawing upon multiple perspectives to tell this story? Do you think one genre is stronger than another?

TECHNIQUE:
The author imagines many conversations between herself and her subject. Clearly, these conversations did not take place. Why does the author choose this rhetorical device and what is gained by using it?

Cecily sometimes "corrects" Lizzie's interpretation. What do you think about this narrative device?

CPSIA information can be obtained
at www.ICGtesting.com
Printed in the USA
LVOW12s0155160117
521073LV00002B/131/P